New Testament Concept of Atonement

The Gospel of the Calvary Event

H.D. McDonald, PLA, DD

The Lutterworth Press
Cambridge

BakerBooks

A Division of Baker Book House Co.
Grand Rapids, Michigan 49516

Dèdicated to Anne, who is more than a Wonderful Wife
— a Co-Partner, Encourager, and Counsellor

Also to

Gràinne and Paul
whose Christian and theological interests are both informed and stimulating

Published in Great Britain 1994 by
The Lutterworth Press
P.O. Box 60
Cambridge
CB1 2NT

Published in the United States 1994 by **Baker Books**
a division of Baker Book House Company
P.O. Box 6287
Grand Rapids
Michigan, 49516-6287

British Library Cataloguing in Publication Data available

Library of Congress Cataloging-in-Publication Data

McDonald, H.D. (Hugh Dermot)
    The New Testament concept of the Atonement: the gospel of
the Calvary event/ H.D. McDonald.
        p. cm.
    ISBN 0-8010-6309-4
      1. Jesus Christ—Crucifixion. 2. Atonement—Biblical teaching
I. Title
BT453.M385 1994
232'.3—dc20   93-16802

Printed in Great Britain by The Guernsey Press Co. Ltd, Guernsey, C.I.

EXPLANATORY PREFACE

There has been a certain compulsion about the writing of this book. It arose out of some remarks made in the many favourable reviews of my 'The Atonement of the Death of Christ' in *Faith, Revelation and History* (Grand Rapids, Baker, 1985). Having myself drawn attention in its introduction to the uneven space given to the three sections - and especially to the limited amount allotted to the biblical as distinct from the historical material - a number of reviewers made the point that they would have welcomed a fuller treatment of the biblical account. So Professor John McIntyre, in his review in the *Expository Times* (June 1987) observed: 'This part of the subject deserves perhaps even fuller treatment in the light of its importance.'

Referring to two controversial issues in the Gospels' teaching on the atonement on which I had refused to comment, Professor McIntyre added, 'that an extended full volume treatment of these would be justified; and one may add appreciated by those who have admiration for Dr McDonald's work.'

It is the opening part of this statement that provided the occasion for my reflection. The latter part must be taken as indicating the gracious spirit of one who has himself contributed much to theological thought, especially in the area of Christology. But his prompting, along with others', compelled me to write something further on the biblical aspect of the atoning significance of Christ's work.

It was not, however, in my mind merely to extend and amplify what I had written in the biblical section of my earlier book. There are, indeed, to hand, volumes enough which detail in fullest measure such data as the New Testament provides. Some different approach was required, which accounts for the method now devised. The present work is not, then, to be regarded just as a supplement to section two of my 'The Atonement of the Death of Christ'. It can stand on its own.

Among the theologians whose writings on the doctrine of the atonement have done most to shape my own thinking the first in rank must be James Denny; followed hard on the heels, and in step, by Emil Brunner and P.T. Forsyth.

Reviewers will doubtless point out a certain repetitiveness in succeeding sections of this book as well as the constant occurrence of certain biblical verses. But these are, I submit, both unavoidable and necessary. In the first place, because repetition is inherent in the biblical literature itself; and in the second, because the single conclusion drawn from any one approach to the Calvary event, whether along the line of its terminology or its interpretation, is that Christ's atoning act is the way of man's redemption. Such repetitions can only be regarded, therefore, as strengthening and confirming the view that Christ's sacrificial death is the sole cause and condition of 'our so great salvation'.

CONTENTS

Explanatory Preface   3

Introduction: The Cruciality of the Cross   7

Note on the Outline   11

   1. The Cross   13

   2. The Tree   23

   3. The Cup   29

   4. The Death   35

   5. The Blood   43

   6. The Body   51

   7. A Lamb Slain   59

   8. A Passover Celebrated   69

   9. A Covenant Made   73

   10. A Sacrifice Rendered   81

   11. A Ransom Paid   89

   12. A Propitiation Offered   97

   13. A Reconciliation Effected   105

   14. Actual Realisation   119

   15. Christological Implications   127

Bibliography   139

Index   141

Introduction
THE CRUCIALITY OF THE CROSS

For the Christian faith questions about God - who he is and what he is like - are ultimately questions about Christ. But questions about Christ become immediately questions about his death and why it is that, according to the New Testament, his death should in some significant way affect God's relation to humanity and to the world.

The followers of Christ were first called Christians at Antioch (Acts 11:26). By their being so called it was recognised that the gospel they preached was centred in him. Since it was common knowledge that Christ had been crucified any reference to him became a reference to him as the one who had been put to death in this terrible way. To speak of Christ at all was, then, to speak of the cross. So Paul simply declares: 'We preach Christ crucified'(1 Cor. 1:23).

The Church's Task

If, therefore, the task of the Church is to proclaim to the world the gospel of God it can only do so by focusing on Christ and his cross. For the gospel of God is one and the same with the gospel of Christ. On seven occasions, beginning with Romans 1:1, it is referred to as 'the gospel of God'; and on another 11, beginning with Mark 1:1, it is designated 'the gospel of Christ'. This conjunction of God and Christ in the gospel, without the least awareness of incongruity, must be read as declaring its origin and procurement as essentially divine. It is in Christ and him crucified that God the creator meets people as the God of their salvation and where individuals experience God through the exercise of saving faith. The deed of God in the Calvary event is, therefore, the place, way and sphere of God's redeeming action, liberating men and women from sin, death and the devil and bringing them into the glorious liberty of the sons of God. It is to Christ's 'sacrifice of atonement' that we owe our whole being as Christians. In the emphatic words of P.T. Forsyth, 'Faith in Christ, in the positive Christian sense, means much more than a relation to God to which Christ supremely helps us. It is a communion not *through*, but only *in* Christ and him crucified.'[1]

However, on the plane of human history, the circumstantial happenings of the Calvary event were darkly characteristic of people's natural reaction to the presence among them of a life of challenging goodness which confronts evil in a way which goes far beyond the limits commonly considered acceptable. Crucifixion was a quite common practice in our Lord's day. There must have been many occasions when a gibbet was set up at Golgotha; and there, between two convicted criminals, Jesus too was crucified one Friday at noon. The Gospels state the fact of his death quite baldly. They make no attempt to garnish the cross with flowers. They do not try to soften its awful reality. Nothing could be more ignominious, more humiliating, more repellent, than a death like this. To 'the natural man' (1 Cor. 2:14, AV) it seems sheer foolishness to believe that anything of eternal moment was transacted at a place where criminals died by one who himself suffered a criminal's death. To such it seems inconceivable that there could be anything divinely and spiritually significant in the death of one hanged on a tree.

From the very first days of the Church until now there have been many who want a Christianity without the cross. They cannot take a gospel centred on one who was crucified as a common criminal. For George Bernard Shaw 'Christianity is not cross-tianity' and Sir Oliver Lodge ventured to suggest that, 'In my opinion Christians make took much of the death of Christ.' The offence of the cross, the sheer scandal of it, has not ceased. For those who believe that their science and philosophy explain the world without the need of the 'God hypothesis' the gospel of the cross is the ultimate absurdity. Others, who retain some belief in a spiritual dimension to human existence, view Christianity as just one more manifestation of mankind's persistent search for meaning to life. They see the Christian faith as but one religion among other world religions. They may even, as a kind of sop to committed Christians, be prepared to allow that it is the best of the bunch in view of the quality of the life and teaching of its founder.

Apostolic Interpreters
This is not how Christ's apostolic interpreters understood the Christian faith. For them it was focused on Christ and specifically on *Christ* as the one *crucified*. For them the gospel was not a rational theory devised by the humanitarianly inclined for whom its teaching of self-sacrifice for the good of others seemed an inspiring ideal. Nor did they see it as designed to supply the religious instincts of people, by the medium of a priestly ritual, with the means to regulate social relationships. For these first exponents of the Christian faith, who were mostly disciples of Jesus before his crucifixion and thus were in the best position to know his mind, his coming was 'to save his people from their sins' (Matt. 1:21).

That the idea that such a death as he died was for the accomplishing of God's saving purpose could have been spun out of their imaginations is unthinkable. They were Jews who knew that anyone who is hung on a tree is under God's curse (cf Deut. 21:23). It was by divine revelation that Peter confessed on their behalf that Jesus was ' "the Christ, the Son of the living God" ' (Matt. 16:16). Later he was to declare that he 'bore our sins in his own body on the tree' (1 Pet. 2:24). For Peter this was the good news that he preached (1 Pet. 1:25).

For Paul, too, the gospel of the cross, of the Son of God who loved him and gave himself for him (Gal. 2:20), was not received from man. It came as 'a revelation of Jesus Christ' (Gal. 1:12). The cross as standing for the death of Christ was for the Church's first preachers and writers the crux of Christianity. It was at the very heart of the message they declared. And it was so because they were fully persuaded that in the action of the Calvary event God had disclosed his saving purpose to humanity. In the deed of the cross the action of God united with the act of Christ on our behalf and for our sake. The act of Christ was not merely a reflection of, or a substitute for, the act of God. Rather 'God was in Christ reconciling the world to himself in the person of his crucified Son' (2 Cor. 5:19). What God alone could do to bring us back to himself Christ did. The New Testament is emphatic that it is in the atoning sacrifice of the cross that God's salvation comes to humanity.

The gospel of the Calvary event contains the reality of the redemption from the sin which separates man from God. Only in this revelation of redemption is God known as the God of the Bible. As the redemptive purpose of God under the old covenant came to be embodied in written scripture, so now in the dispensation of the new covenant is it enshrined in the far richer and more glorious disclosure of the New Testament. We are bound to scripture for, as Calvin argues,

> since no daily responses are given from heaven, and the Scriptures are the only records in which God has been pleased to consign his truth to perpetual remembrance, the full authority which they ought to possess with the faithful is not recognized, unless they are believed to have come from heaven, as directly as if God had been heard giving utterance to them.[2]

The biblical revelation thus centres on the Christ of the cross and the cross of Christ as its essential content. It is through the biblical revelation that God's redemptive act is brought home to faith, for Christ's death is more than a historical happening. For God, who acted in time and yet transcends time, is ever present for man's salvation in the divine action of the cross. The work of Christ thus presently experienced lifts God's reconciling act at Calvary above the realm of the historical, whilst it is itself firmly anchored in history.

The cross of Golgatha is the site of our redemption and the message of Christ crucified is both the heart of the gospel and the focus of the whole of scripture. Accordingly this book is about the centrality and cruciality of the cross of Christ.

Notes

1. Forsyth, P.T., (1909) *The Person and Place of Jesus Christ*, London, Hodder & Stoughton, 6.
2. Calvin, J., *The Institutes of the Christian Religion*, tr. (1940) by Beveridge, Henry, London, James Clarke, i, 68.

NOTE ON OUTLINE

There are a number of single words in the New Testament each of which holds in itself something of the essential meaning and message of the Christian doctrine of salvation as actualized in the death of Christ. Some of these terms, like the 'blood' and the 'death' are distinctly related to his person. Others, though in themselves neutral or physical, like that of the 'tree' and the 'cup' by a metonyming acquire a personal character through their association with Christ's redeeming activity. It seems necessary, consequently, for a fuller account of that redeeming activity to explore the biblical usage of these terms in their connection with the Calvary event. In the first part of this book (Chapters I-VI) we shall begin our investigation with those terms which are less personal and proceed to those which are more specifically so.

The second part of the book (Chapters VII-XIII) will look at the various biblical interpretations of the Calvary event.

The final two chapters will take into account the results of this detailed survey, and examine its implications for Christology.

Chapter I
THE CROSS

The cross has become for the church the universal symbol of Christianity. But it was not so from the first. Other symbols were prior to it, such as the dove, the fish, and ark, as can be seen on the walls of the catacombs outside Rome. But these symbols are, for the most part, accidental and peripheral; they do not, that is to say, symbolise the essential reality of the Christian gospel. They do not get to the true heart and soul of it. The fact is that in the first days of Christianity, as it spread throughout the Roman empire, the symbol of the cross was avoided. To have displayed it would have been regarded as raising the standard of rebellion and attempting to displace the symbols of the emperor's divinity and authority with the sign of another king. The immediate reaction by the state would have been a fresh round of persecution of Christians. Thus it was that 'the cross, now the universal symbol of Christianity, was at first avoided, not only for its direct association with Christ, but for its shameful association with the execution of common criminals also.'[1] As, however, Christianity spread and was declared by Constantine to be the official religion of the empire, the cross came more and more into prominence as the accepted symbol of the faith.

As a symbol, however, the cross may be either empty or eloquent. Empty, if a cross as a mere material thing is thought to possess in itself some magical power. In the second century there arose the superstitious notion that a wooden cross could be used to ward off evil spirits. For some people, reared in a religious tradition where physical images hold a large place, a cross has come to be regarded almost as a good luck charm. So much has been made of the actual physical cross in some quarters of the church that, were there collected from the churches and cathedrals of Christendom all the wood claimed as parts of the true cross, it would make a load too heavy for Simon the Cyrenean to have carried up Golgotha's hill. Only too easily, it would seem, can the symbol itself be taken as the substance and mere religious drapery as the true reality.

There are times when true believers need to be reminded that sensory symbols are at best, like the ritual acts of the old economy, mere shadows of the true. There is no need for such physical signs or sensory symbols to bolster faith. Nor would faith be any the more confirmed if, for example, it were announced that the roll from which Jesus read the words of Isaiah in the synagogue of Nazareth (Luke 4:16f.), as fulfilled in himself, had been found; nor that the boat in which he sat to teach the people (Mark 4:1f.) had been discovered; nor that the towel with which he wiped the disciples' feet had been unearthed (John 13:4): for we have a word authenticated by the Holy Spirit's inspiration which affirms that he did all these things; and that is enough for faith. Faith is not made any the more credible to unbelievers nor is it the more strengthened in believers if it were proved to be so. True, in the gospels there is the record of a woman healed by touching the hem of Christ's garment (Matt. 9:20; cf. 14:36); but it was not any magic property in the garment, *per se*, that brought about the miracle. It was from Christ himself that the virtue went forth (Mark 5:30; cf. Luke 6:19 and 8:46).

Yet for those who are helped by such visual aids, a cross may have an eloquent voice. A cross on a church spire could be for its people a reminder that the church exists only because of the cross of Christ. So, too, a cross on the communion table could be a reminder to those who gather to its celebration that it is because of the blood of the cross they have remission of sins. And a cross above, or carved into, the pulpit could be a reminder to the preacher and people alike that the gospel centres in the proclamation of Christ and him crucified.

But such crosses on the church spire, the communion table and the pulpit are too smooth, too polished, too ornate by far, to convey the least idea of what death on a cross was like. It was a shameful thing to be crucified: it was a criminal's death. We have decked the cross too much with flowers and hidden beneath them its harsh and horrible reality. To die on a cross was to be accursed. We have turned the cross from a thing so nasty to a thing too nice. We have almost made the cross respectable; elevated it to a lovely modern and inspiring symbol. But the cross on Calvary hill was nothing such. Death on a cross was an awful way to terminate a human life, reserved only for the worst of criminals. It was the severest punishment meted out to recalcitrant slaves and villainous robbers. The passion account of the crucifixion of Jesus, as recorded in the four Gospels, has all the horrific details of Roman executions: the jeering crowds; the scourging of the victim; the accusations written above; and all the pains and wounding in the body and spirit of the one nailed fast to the gibbet. It was because of the false charges made against him by the rulers of Israel that Jesus was publicly crucified by the Romans. Crucifixion as a method of carrying out the sentence of death on one condemned was not favoured by the Jews; they left it to the occupying authorities to carry out the deed. For the Romans there was no religious significance attached to the cross. They regarded crucifixion as merely an instrument for inflicting the most degrading form of judicial punishment. But if the Jews spurned crucifixion, Christians saw in the Hebrew prophetic scriptures suggestions of his crucifixion in the uplifted serpent of Numbers 21:8-9 (cf. John 3:14) and the pierced hands and feet of Psalm 22:16 (cf. John 19:37).

There are 11 references to the cross in the passion stories as recorded in the four Gospels. For it is with a real event, an actual historic cross, that the gospel is concerned. It is the cross on Golgotha, and not a symbolic cross, that is God's means of human redemption. At the Calvary scene itself some came to an awareness that there was something distinctive about the cross of Jesus the Galilean. There was something of eternal moment, something specifically divine, about it which set it apart from every other cross of crucifixion set up at Golgotha. On the cross was one of whom Pilate had confessed, ' "I find no crime in him".' (John 19:6.) Of him a centurion testified, ' "Certainly this man was innocent!" ' (Luke 23:47), and ' "Truly this was the son of God!" ' (Mat. 27:54). Even the scoffing rulers had to confess, ' "He saved others" ' (Luke 23:35). And he who was transfixed had himself declared before Pilate, ' "You would have no power over me unless it had been given you from above" ' (John 19:11). One was there on the cross who in the agony of his ignominious crucifixion appealed to God as Father, ' "Father, forgive them; for they know not what they do" ' (Luke 23:34). One was there on the cross who in his last dying moments spoke with a loud voice, ' "Father, into thy hands I commend my spirit!" ' (Luke 23:46). Those words, spoken with a loud voice of certain confidence and sovereignty, must have called to the minds of some of those present at Calvary who had human sympathy and spiritual insight the words of Ecclesiastes 8:8, 'No man has power to retain the spirit, or authority over the day of death.' He who hung there had that power for he had previously told his disciples that he had the right to lay down his life and to take it again (John 10:18; cf. 18:11). It was open to those who heard him speak out his words as he dismissed his spirit on the cross to draw the conclusion that something was happening in which God and not just man was intimately present.

But if the full import and right conclusion of those affirmations at the cross and from it did not dawn upon those spectators at the scene, they were certainly brought home to Paul the apostle by the Holy Spirit's inspiration. To Paul we owe the fullest statement of the meaning and message of the gospel of the cross. When Paul wrote his epistles it was not in front of a cross adorning his study desk to remind him of Calvary. In his prison cell he did not need any such symbolic cross when he wrote to the people of God. For him, the cross - the event of Calvary - was ever in his vision, his heart, his gospel. He could not himself forget, nor will he let it ever be forgotten, that the cross was in fact, a terrible reality. And it was on that cross on the site of

Golgotha where he knew God's deed for the salvation of man was done. It was back to the cross he looked; back to what man did there to the Lord of glory. From there too he looked up to what God did through the Lord of glory for the redemption of sinners. The cross was not for Paul a nice religious symbol of a lovely myth. It was not for Paul the stimulus or focus of a religious mysticism. Paul had a clear and open message of the cross based squarely on the historic event of Calvary. Yet for Paul the historic cross as such was not the focus of his gospel; but the historic cross in its divine meaning as God's way of redemption. Thus did the cross mean for Paul that God, 'as the Forgiving One, really comes to sinful man.'[2]

Ten times in his epistles Paul makes use of the term 'the cross' to declare its place and purpose in God's scheme of redemption (cf. 1 Cor. 1:17-18; Gal. 5:11-12; 6:14, Eph. 2:16; Phil. 2:8; 3:18; Col. 1:20; 2:14). All of these statements make it evident that God comes to man in the abiding reality and efficacy of the cross of Christ. For Paul the cross was the centre of the apostolic gospel. His interest in the cross was neither archaeological nor historical, but in what God did in Christ on the cross personally, racially and cosmically.

Reconciliation

Our concern at the moment is with the cross as the means of reconciliation. Later I will discuss the nature of reconciliation accomplished on the cross. Inevitably, some statements which must be made here will be repeated then to make evident the object and range of reconciliation brought about by God's redeeming act in the Calvary event.

It is 'by the blood of the cross' that God has made peace through Christ to 'reconcile to himself all things, whether on earth or in heaven' (Col. 1:20). Paul does not state specifically what is to be understood by the 'all things on earth or in heaven' which are reconciled 'by the blood of his cross'. It would, however, seem right to refer the 'all things' of this reconciliation to the 'all things created' of the same chapter (vv. 16-17) but perhaps it is not necessary to be too precise. For Paul was so taken up with the truth, so transparent and wonderful, of the reconciliation achieved by the cross of Christ that he could conceive of no limit to its scope. Wherever the estranging condition of sin is felt, whether in the seen or unseen world, the blood of the cross is the way of its reconciliation. However radically the cosmic order was disturbed by sin (Rom. 8:20), it is still with sin and its effects that the efficacious action of the blood of the cross deals. Paul does not actually refer in Colossians to the process by which man finds reconciliation to his cosmic existence, yet by making peace through the blood of the cross to reconcile 'all things' to himself, for the believer there must be reconciliation to God's providential order and peaceful acceptance of the conditions of his human lot.

Some commentators on Colossians are more specific about the object of the reconciliation by the blood of Christ's cross. They would refer it to the principalities and powers of the next chapter (cf. 2:15), and thus explain the reconciliation as their 'disarming', making them a public spectacle by his triumph over them in the cross. This is admitted to be a strange use of the word 'reconciled', but when associated with the idea of 'making peace' as in 1:20 it can be held to yield the idea of 'pacification'. By their defeat at the cross the principalities and powers which hold hostile sway in the world have been pacified. At the beginning of Jesus' ministry the devil offered him lordship over the kingdoms of the world if he would fall down and worship him (Matt. 4:9; Luke 4:7). But Jesus resisted the temptation, for he was already aware that he had come into the world to destroy the works of the devil, and through the cross God would reconcile the world to himself in him.

The racial reconciliation achieved by the cross is stated in Ephesians 2:16. The enmity which divided Jew and Gentile was slain in the cross and access gained for both in one *Spirit* to the Father (cf. 2:16-18). In 'the blood of Christ' (v. 13), 'in his flesh' (v. 15), 'through the cross' (v. 16) is the reconciliation achieved. In Christ the dividing wall of hostility between Jew and Gentile was broken down: the spiritual barrier has been set aside so that the physical obstruction has become meaningless. The veil of the temple has been torn asunder from top to bottom (Matt. 27:51). Only by God in the cross of Christ could the barrier of hostility be removed and both Jew and Gentile come together as one holy temple in the Lord (v.21).

Although the cross is specifically related, in Ephesians, to the reconciliation of Jew and Gentile - 'us both' - this is but an instance of that more fundamental reconciliation effected by Christ between God and man. It is by the cross that peace with God is established (Col. 1:20); and it is in the cross that the catalogue of man's sin is taken away (Col. 2:14). Christ in his death cancelled the bond which stood against us with its legal demands, setting it aside by nailing it to the cross. Against us stood the demands of the law as a certificate of our indebtedness, its requirements unfulfilled and our indebtedness unpaid, the terrifying instrument of our condemnation. Such was the bond Christ 'set aside', nullifying the terms of its judgement by nailing it to his cross. The suggestion that there was an ancient custom of nailing up the cancelled bond has no great support; nor has that of the nailing up of a trophy above the conqueror's head although both ideas would fit well the thought enshrined in the words. More weight can be given to the view that a scroll of the victim's misdeeds was nailed above his head on the crucifixion gibbet (cf. Mark 15:26). But whatever the particular allusion, one fact is clear: all that stood in the way of our acceptance by God has been done away by the cross. On the cross Christ did all that was necessary for us, to all that was against us, so that we might be forgiven all our trespasses (Col. 2:13). He took away the scroll of our condemnation that hung above our heads. By his death the document of legal charge against us is swept aside. 'Because Christ was nailed to the cross in our stead, the debt is forgiven.'[3]

Paul uses strong words for the effectiveness of the cross as 'the instrument of our merciful deliverance'.[4] The writing having been erased (cf. Acts 3:19), the document itself was torn up and thrown away (cf. 2 Thess. 2:7). So has God blotted out our transgressions, to remember our sins no more (Isa. 43:25; 44:22; Jer. 31:34).

> Christ has wiped the slate clean and given us a fresh start. He took the signed confession of our indebtedness which stood as a perpetual witness against us, and cancelled it by his death; you might actually say he took the document, ordinance and all, and nailed it to his cross as an act of triumphant defiance in the face of those blackmailing powers who were holding it over us as a threat.[5]

By a completed act Christ has dealt with the sin question in the Calvary event. For there he 'has (in accord with current practice of re-using expensive papyrus) washed the gum and soot ink marks from the document; he has taken it out of our way; and he nailed it up publicly, as so cancelled upon his cross.'[6]

Gathered around this one word the 'cross' are all the saving realities of Christ's atoning death. The cross, which had seemed to the two disciples on the Emmaus road the destruction of their hopes (Luke 24:21), had now become the actualised divine event of man's salvation. Thus is 'the word of the cross' (1 Cor. 1:18), which is identified in the previous verse with the proclamation of the gospel, the redemptive message for mankind. And in the cross alone will Paul glory (Gal. 6:14). Others may 'boast' in 'the flesh'; for Paul it will be 'in the cross'. Those of the circumcision might feast their eyes on the mutilated flesh of their deluded converts. Paul's gaze will be on the torn figure of him who in his body bore his sins to the tree. Paul set before his eyes Christ and him crucified. Such a one, the Lord Jesus Christ, was nailed to the cross by the hands of sinners, but he was held there by a love divine (Gal. 2:20). Paul reminds the Galatians of what they knew already, the saving energy of the cross. Yet in stating it again he would arouse them to a fresh appreciation of the cross, and recall to them how gladly they had accepted what had been done for them in the deed of the cross, as the all-sufficient way of their full salvation.

There was, of course, a shame in what Jesus underwent when he suffered on the cross as a common criminal. And to the natural man, unconcerned about sin, the word of the cross is sheer folly (2 Cor. 1:18). The Jews considered as accursed one whose dead body hung upon a gibbet. But it was our curse that was fastened on Jesus (Gal. 3:13). In Hebrews 12:2, as in Philippians 2:8, the word for the cross is used without the article, according to Westcott, 'in order to fix attention on the nature of the death'.[7] In the passage in Philippians 'cross' is to express what was the ultimate scandal for the religious Jew and the rational Greek (cf. 1 Cor. 1:22). 'Even to death on a cross', was the lowest stage in Christ's humiliation from his prior state of equality with God (Phil. 2:6 8). In his obedience unto death Christ reached the bottom rung of the ladder that led down from the throne of God. The cross had, however, for Christ its side of glory. For he who had come from the highest (Phil. 2:6) and descended to the lowest (Phil. 2:8) is from the cross highly exalted to be confessed as 'Lord, to the glory of God the Father' (Phil. 2:11). It is in truth through the resurrection that the atonement of the cross is made real and realisable within the faith of the church. For it is not the Christ of the historic cross as an event in the distant past, vital and necessary as that is, but Christ the living Lord who, in virtue of his death, assures forgiveness of our sins and the restoration of our souls. While the cross made the atonement actual, it is the resurrection that makes it experiential; for the atoning efficacy of the cross is given perpetual efficacy by the resurrection.

The affirmations drawn out from those who stood within the shadow of the cross are given new significance as the cross is made real and realisable by the resurrection. To Pilate's, "I find no fault in him" the inspired writers respond: it was so, for it was a sinless Christ that was nailed to the cross (1 Pet. 2:22; 2 Cor. 5:21). Yet it was such who bore our sin in his body on the tree (2 Pet. 2:24), and 'for sin, he condemned sin in the flesh' (Rom. 8:3). Said a centurion, "Certainly this was a righteous man". He was indeed so, responds the apostle Peter, for he endured the cross as the 'righteous for the unrighteous, that he might bring us to God' (1 Pet. 3:18; cf. 2 Cor. 5:21; 1 John 2:1). The same centurion exclaimed, "Truly this was a son of God!" Certainly, declares the inspired Paul, for he was 'the Son of God, who loved me, and gave himself for me'. (Gal. 2:20). And John adds that 'the blood of Jesus his [God's] Son cleanses us from all sin' (1 John 1:7). The rulers mocked, "he saved others, himself he cannot save". To which the New Testament writers respond: he cannot save himself; he cannot - because he would not. For it was precisely in not choosing to save himself, in electing not to preserve his own life, but in giving it, that he would save others.

All the confessions drawn out regarding him during the days of the passion were true of him who endured the cross; and all that was true of him went to make the cross the means of man's salvation. The one thing that matters for sinners is that it has really taken place. But if it has really happened, then it has happened once for all. Historical humanity as a whole is the object of the divine healing. All that is called history is included in it; only thus is it really the Cross of Christ.[8]

The Cross in John's Gospel

There are three places in the fourth Gospel where the phrase 'lifted up' occurs (John 3:14; 8:28; 12:34) as a synonym for the cross. The word was, indeed, in currency virtually as a technical one for crucifixion. By implication it is used of Christ's death in 3:14, but in 12:33-4 the reference to it is clear. Some commentators take the phrase, especially in 12:32, to refer to Christ's ascension on the strength of the words 'from the earth', reading them as 'above the earth'. Westcott goes further and declares that the original Greek phrase (*ek tes ges*) expresses not only 'above the earth' but 'out of the earth as taken from the sphere of action'. He sees, therefore, a reference, not primarily to the crucifixion, but particularly to the resurrection and exaltation. Lightfoot considers that the two ideas of crucifixion and exaltation combine in the words. 'The lifting up must be understood in the twofold meaning, each side being rigorously maintained.' He adds, however, that the exaltation 'has its central feature in his death'.[9] For my part, however, the phrase here, as in its other two occurrences, I regard as referring specifically to Christ's 'lifting up' on the cross. The serpent in the wilderness was certainly not lifted out of the sight of the people, but set on an elevation to be seen by all.

Moses' setting up a serpent on a pole (Num. 21:4ff.) - representing the serpents by which the people were plagued by the Lord for their sins (v. 7) - shadowed forth Christ's 'lifting up' for man's sin. By linking his 'lifting up' with the elevated serpent in the wilderness, the evangelist leaves us in no doubt that the allusion is to the cross as the instrument of salvation. Plagued by serpents because of their sin, the people were instructed to see in the uplifted serpent transfixed to the pole the means of their sins' cancellation and their healing from the wounds of the serpents. For the stricken lives of men to be healed it was necessary for Christ to go to the cross. As Moses lifted up the serpent in the wilderness, so must [*dei* - 'it is necessary'] the son of man be lifted up' (John 3:14). And in his being 'lifted up' he was made the very thing that the Old Serpent has brought to man - sin. He who knew no sin was on the cross, 'made sin' on our behalf. Thus by his cross did Christ the Redeemer bruise the serpent's head (cf. Gen. 3:15). There did the 'ancient serpent, who is the Devil and Satan' (Rev. 20:2) suffer defeat. In the cross Christ took upon himself all the human sin of which the devil was originator and mankind the propagator, and there he destroyed the devil's power and cancelled man's guilt. Therefore, neither must the church nor the preachers of the church's gospel, lose the revelation of it by reducing it to a symbol, like the cross or dogma . . . we must keep before ourselves and others the concrete facts in which the reality first came home to men. Christ crucified must be 'evidently set forth' - placarded(Gal. 3:1 AV) before men's eyes - that they may receive a due impression of all there is in this wonderful sight.[9]

The Jews had not considered this 'lifting up,' this cross, to be the lot of the Messiah when he came. They had been taught that when he came he would be with them forever. When, therefore, Jesus of Galilee, whom some had come to believe to be the Messiah, was heard to speak of his being 'lifted up' they were perplexed. They posed the question, ' "We have heard from the law that the Christ remains forever. How can you say that the Son of man must be lifted up? Who is this Son of man?" ' (John 12:34). They had yet to learn that only by way of the cross could he fulfil the messianic role; only in the cross would the messianic role as prophesied by Isaiah 53 be fulfilled. Only, indeed, as one who had been crucified could he remain with his people forever. It is in the gospel of the cross that the new society of the redeemed is constituted. For it is as the Son of man is 'lifted up' that he draws to himself 'a chosen race, a royal priesthood, a holy nation, God's own people' (1 Pet. 2:9), the new 'Israel of God' (Gal. 6:16). Thus the cross is the potent, the majestic factor in the Christian gospel. In the light of the cross, God is understood for the God that he is, a God of justice and love 'who gave his only beloved son' to the death of the cross. And this for the judgement of sin once for all, and the revelation of his love in him everlastingly.

It remains to notice here, as a kind of appendix, Luther's contention that the cross is the touchstone of all theological reflection. For Luther, the cross is conceived not only as the essential factor of Christ's work for man's salvation but, even more, as rooted in the total plan of God's self-disclosure. Luther's theology of the cross consciously opposed the '*theologia crucis*' to the '*theologia gloriae*' - the 'theology of glory' - of later medieval scholasticism. The basic issue concerned the absoluteness of the revealed knowledge of God against the tentative nature of natural theology. Luther perceived the cross as both the centre and circumference of Christian theology. It does not only occupy the apex of the biblical revelation, but no less decisively forms its foundation and the keystone of its arch. In Luther's view God is known and understood only in the cross.

The *theologia gloriae* would locate the 'thatness' of God, his existence, wisdom, power and goodness, in the presence and orderliness of creation. By contrast, Luther, while allowing a certain significance to natural theology, contends that God's certainty and reality, his essential 'whatness', is hidden in the suffering and humiliation of the cross, to be disclosed only to faith. The protagonists of a natural theology - the *theologia gloriae* - declare that it belongs to rational human ability to discover God's presence in the moral and physical cosmic order. Such a claim, Luther responds, must lead inevitably to that human pride which is the antithesis of the humility and contrition required of man before God, to which alone is disclosed God's saving knowledge in the humiliation and god-forsakenness of the cross of Christ.

Notes

1. Gough, M., (1973) *The Origins of Christian Art*, London, Thames & Hudson, 20.
2. Brunner, E., (1934) *The Mediator*, tr. Wyon, O., London, Lutterworth, 506.
3. Lohse, E., (1971)*A Commentary on the Epistle to the Colossians and Philemon* ed. Koester, Helmut, Philadelphia, Fortress Press.
4. Moule, H.C.G., (1898) *Colossians Studies*, London, Hodder & Stoughton.
5. Simpson, E.K. and Bruce, F.F., (1951) *Commentary on Ephesians and Colossians, New International Commentary*, ed. Bruce, F.F. Grand Rapids, Eerdmans.
6. White, R.E.O., (1970) *Broadman Bible Commentary*, ed. Allen, Clifton J., Nashville, Broadman Press.
7. Westcott, B.F., (1890) *The Epistle to the Hebrews*, London, MacMillan.
8. Brunner, *op. cit.*, 506, 508.
9. Lightfoot, R.H., (1956)*St. John's Gospel: A Commentary*, Revised Edition, ed. Evans, C.F., Oxford, OUP, 243.
10. Denney, James, (1911) *The Christian Doctrine of Reconciliation*, London, Hodder & Stoughton, 18.

Chapter II
THE TREE

The apostle Peter does not use the term 'cross' in connection with Christ's death. But on three occasions he speaks of Christ's hanging on a 'tree', twice as the way of his crucifixion (Acts 5:30; 10:39), and once in relation to his saving work (1 Pet. 2:24). Paul uses the same expression in his address in the synagogue of Antioch of Pisidia in connection with Christ's treatment at the hands of the rulers. He declares: ' "And when they had fulfilled all that was written of him, they took him down from the tree, and laid him in a tomb" '(Acts 13:29). In Galatians 3:13 he quotes the Old Testament passage, 'Cursed be everyone who hangs on a tree' as having its analogical fulfilment in Christ's death on the cross.

The word translated 'tree' in all these references is not the usual one for a tree in growth, *dendron*. The Greek *xulon* of the texts which is translated simply as 'wood' in some New Testament passages (cf. Luke 23:31, 1 Cor. 23:12; Rev. 18:12) connotes rather a rough piece of wood. But in connection with the act of crucifixion the wood refers to a beam from which someone is suspended as with Christ on the cross. In Acts 16:24 *xulon* is translated 'stocks', and refers to clamps into which a prisoner's feet were thrust and fastened with thongs (cf. Job 13:27; 33:11). In its plural form the word appears in connection with the scourging of Jesus at the time of the crucifixion and is translated 'clubs' in the synoptic Gospels (Matt. 26:47,55; Mark 14:43,48; Luke 22:52). *Xulon*, then, would seem to be the blanket term for all the grim implements of a crucifixion. The 'wood' of the scourging and the 'wood' on which the condemned was transfixed, a piece of rough and unpolished timber hurriedly laid hold upon for the brutal occasion. Peter, who was present recalled the event: Jesus 'crucified and killed by the hands of lawless men' (Acts 2:23) by being hung on a *xulon*.

Peter and the Cross
Yet for Peter the hanging of Christ on a tree, which at the time must have seemed the most tragic and incomprehensible of human acts, was now, in the light of Christ's resurrection, an event which took place 'according to the definite plan and foreknowledge of God'. Right at the beginning of the church's life, Peter, in the first Christian sermon, fastens on the death of

Christ as significant for Christ's saving work for the forgiveness of sins. He views the death of Christ on the 'tree' from two sides: the manward and the Godward. It was a crime on the part of humanity, of Jews and Romans alike. For although the Jews could find in him nothing worthy of death, yet they saw to it that Pilate would have him crucified (Acts 13:28). On the other hand, the Calvary event was within God's purpose. So Christ's death was no surprise to God nor indeed to Christ himself. It was neither an unfortunate incident nor an unforeseen accident. The ending of Christ's life on a tree was in fulfilment of 'all that was written of him', says Paul (Acts 13:29; cf. 1 Cor. 15:3). These statements at once link Christ's death on the tree with the prophetic declaration he himself made that he must suffer and be killed (Matt. 16:21). The fact of his death was, then, a part of, indeed. more truly the absolute means of God's pardon of sinners. It was, consequently, in the name of him who died that divine forgiveness was proclaimed. The apostolic preachers of the earliest church saw this significance of Christ's death vindicated by his being raised from the dead (Acts 10:40; 13:30).

It is claimed by some that the apostolic witnesses were so concerned to establish that the Messiah does indeed 'live forever' that they hardly dared mention his death, which they saw as an unhappy incident soon put right by God's decisive act of resurrection. Only later, it is suggested, did they find some rationale for it. This interpretation cannot for a moment be accepted. For one thing, these men had already learned from Christ himself that he must suffer at the hands of wicked men; and they had learned, too, that there was a divine purpose in his being 'killed'. His being 'killed' was not because of a human conspiracy from which he saw no way of escape: for he had, on his own account, laid down his life in a voluntary act for the ransom of many. There was no power of man that could have nailed him to the wood of the cross except it were allowed of God (John 19:11). All these things his apostolic band had heard from him; and now, in the aftermath of Pentecost, by the Spirit's action they would be brought back to mind as they gave an understanding of the saving significance of the Calvary event (John 16:13). And those disciples had, besides, sat with him at the Last Supper and heard him speak about his body broken and blood shed for the remission of sins. They would not, therefore, in the light of the resurrection, fail to connect his death on the tree with the gospel of forgiveness they were commissioned to proclaim.

It is, of course, to be granted that the full meaning of the Calvary event as God's atoning act in Christ was not disclosed to Peter at the beginning. At first it was the reality of the crucifixion of Jesus, who he had once confessed as the Messiah, the Son of the living God (Matt. 16:16), that appalled him and compelled his recognition that such a deed could not be outside God's reconciling purpose for mankind. When, therefore, he wrote his epistle, Peter's thought had turned from the crucifixion as an act of man to the one crucified's being on the tree as the work of God. Thus was the truth brought home to him that there Christ bore our sins in his body (1 Pet. 3:18) through the shedding of his blood as of a lamb without blemish or spot (1:19).

There is no more definite statement about the atoning work of Christ in all the New Testament than that in 1 Peter 2:24. Every word in the verse is heavy with significance. It was 'he himself' who 'bore our sins'; no less, and no other, than he, 'our Lord Jesus Christ' (1:3), 'the righteous one' (3:18). He took our sins upon himself (Num. 4:33) and there they perished. Our sins he bore 'in his body'. He carried up the whole intolerable weight of the world's iniquity to the gibbet of crucifixion. There he transfixed their terrible catalogue in his body to the wood of the 'accursed tree'.

In its every affirmation this verse echoes the prophecy of Isaiah 53. 'He himself bore our sins in his body to the tree, that we might die to sin and live to righteousness. By his wounds you have been healed.' (1 Pet. 2:24) A targum on Isaiah 53:10 is an illuminating commentary on Peter's words: 'and from before Jehovah it was the will to refine and purify the remnant of his people that he might cleanse from sins their souls; that they might see the kingdom of his Christ . . . and prolong their days.' He bore our sins: the Lord hath laid on him the iniquity of us all. Numbered with transgressors yet he bore the sins of many and made intercession for the transgressors. He was delivered from death, that as the living one he might 'see his seed', 'the fruit of the travail of his soul', in lives redeemed from death in his death. Peter's final declaration in this verse, 'by his wounds you have been healed' is a direct quotation from Isaiah 53:5.

Peter's references to Christ's being hanged on a tree are linked to his resurrection from the dead. This is the passage of Christ's atoning work via the tree to the throne. It is of significance, therefore, that the word for 'tree' (1 Pet. 2:24), *xulon* is the same as that used by John in the Revelation for the 'tree of life' (Rev. 2:7; 22:2,19). It is not being too fanciful to suggest that it is in the atonement of the tree of the crucified that there was opened for mankind a way to eat of the tree of life. The death he died for us was to pay the price of sin so that there might be given to faith the gift of God which is eternal life (Rom. 5:21; cf. 3:22-26). In Revelation 22:1-2, the two expressions 'the lamb' and 'the tree' which appear in Peter's epistle occur in juxtaposition. For John, as for Peter, it is the Lamb slain (Rev. 5:6,8,12; 6:1; 13:8), the crucified who is the 'tree of life'.

Peter's words in 1 Peter 2:24 on the significance of the Calvary event come in the context of a consideration of the suffering being endured by his readers as followers of Christ. In 2:19-25 he counsels them patiently to endure it as approved by God, 'because Christ also suffered for you, leaving you an example that you should follow in his steps'. Christ in his sufferings 'trusted to him who judges justly', and in that spirit the believer is to bear his sufferings after the example of Christ. Returning to the same theme in chapter 3 he speaks of a certain blessedness which comes to those who suffer for righteousness' sake (v. 17). And it is better to suffer for doing right, if that should be the will of God, than for doing wrong. But while in both chapters Peter presents Christ's attitude and spirit in suffering as an example and inspiration for those who suffer, he immediately in both chapters goes beyond this application to indicate a significant difference between the sufferings he endured and what his readers do or may do. In his case he did not suffer even for doing right, as the immediate context would lead us to expect. His word is rather that he suffered for sins, as if to turn their thought from a merely exemplarist and inspirationalist view of Christ's work to its ultimate redemptive nature. 'For Christ suffered for sins once for all, the righteous for the unrighteous.' That brings Christ's suffering into another dimension. On the level of human endurance the sufferings of Christ are, of course, an example and inspiration to the believer. Nevertheless, in the divine purpose his sufferings were of a different order. Christ did not suffer for evil doings of his own, for he knew no sin; nor were his sufferings, like those of Peter's readers, for doing right. His sufferings were unique, an atoning sacrifice for sin.

The Cross in Paul

The apostle Paul refers in Galatians 3:13 to the tree in a quotation from Deuteronomy 21:23: 'Christ redeemed us from the curse of the law, having become a curse for us - for it is written, "Cursed is everyone that hangs on a tree". The verse comes in without an introduction to bring Christ into the tragic scene of man's condemnation under the law and consequently by the law 'cursed'. To the curse of the law all are in bondage; but from the 'curse' Christ has brought man out of, being made, in a profound and actual sense, 'a curse' for us. Man is made free from the curse of the law's condemnation by Christ's 'curse-bearing' death. It is understandable that some early commentators of the medieval church, following Jerome, moved away from the plain sense of the passage by refusing to allow that it could be Christ who is the one cursed by hanging on a tree. This called down the wrath of Luther in his comment on the passage in his *Epistle to the Galatians*. Certainly it is of Christ that the statement is made. He most surely knew the awful capacity of sin to bring about separation from God (cf. Matt. 27:46) by being subjected himself to the curse and condemnation of the law.

In the statement the emphasis falls on the word 'Christ': he it is who redeemed us from the curse of the law. This he did by 'having become a curse for us'. As Luther in his commentary declares, Paul did not say that,

> Christ was made a curse for himself, but for us. Therefore all the weight stands on the word 'for us'. For Christ was innocent as concerning his own person, and therefore he ought not to have been hanged on a tree ... [yet] Christ also according to the law ought to be hanged for he sustained the person of a sinner and of a thief, not of one but of many sinners and thieves. For we are sinners and thieves and guilty of death and guilty of eternal damnation. But Christ took all our sins upon himself and for them died on the cross: therefore it behoves that he become a transgressor (and as Isaiah the prophet saith, chapter 53) 'to be reckoned and numbered among transgressors and trespassers'.[1]

Becoming 'a curse for us' is, indeed, a strong and startling statement. For Christ became himself that very thing the law made us - 'a curse'. So identified was he with sinful humanity that all that is of sinful humanity became his; actually and literally his. The law brought him under the curse; and he brought himself under it, and made the curse of the law his own. The thought echoes the idea of the scapegoat and burnt offerings of Leviticus 5:5f., in which the victim is regarded as bearing the sins of all for whom atonement is made. The curse is transferred from them to it; and it becomes in very actuality the impersonation of the sin and the curse (cf. 2 Cor. 5:21). Thus did Christ become what we are in all the realness and fullness of it. He experienced in himself the law's dark threatenings and all God's awful condemnation by becoming himself the object of the divine wrath as one by the law accursed. For as one 'accursed' he was hanged on a tree. In taking the curse that was ours on himself Christ by his own self-dedication submitted to the law's condemnation, and thus to the wrath and judgement of God on sin. 'So the curse', says Luther, 'which is the wrath of God, was meted out on him, and so God hath laid our sins, not on us, but upon his Son, Christ, that he bearing the punishment thereof, might be our peace'.[2]

Paul omits from his quotation from Deuteronomy 21:23 the words 'accursed of God' which are found in the Hebrew and Septuagint text, although there are good reasons for regarding the words a authentic. There is a genuine sense, however, in which the words (which are in brackets in the AV although retained in the RSV) could have stood, for the Messiah, in the prophetic words of Isaiah was indeed 'smitten by God, and afflicted' (Isa. 53:4). What, however, stands out in the passage is the fact that Christ in his death as 'one accursed' wrought salvation for mankind. The 'curse' that he became 'for us' is not to be regarded as an independent operative principle. It is God's holy judgement on man's sin which he had to undergo instead of us. Paul does not state in specific terms *how* Christ's death on the tree, as one accursed, effected our reconciliation. What, however, he does make certain is that God made the punishment, which Christ took voluntarily upon himself, valid for his own right to deal with man in grace. Such a redemption accomplished on the tree of sacrifice does not wear the aspect of a neat transaction, a nice balancing of the active and passive voice. It comes rather with a feeling of mystery, yet, at the same time, with a sense of adequacy, in which blend the reality and integrity of God's holy justice and love coming to their fullest expression in the Calvary event of the tree of crucifixion.

In this regard the fundamental truth apropos Golgotha's 'tree' is formed in quaint language in stanza xxiii of St John of the Cross's *Canticle*, entitled 'Beneath the Apple-tree'. There it is declared his soul was betrothed to his beloved: and there did he know something of the soul's redemption. The exposition following runs like this:

The Spouse sets forth to the soul in this stanza the wondrous manner of His redemption of her and of His betrothal of her to Himself, using the same terms to describe the corruption and ruin of the human race, and saying that, even as by means of the forbidden tree of Paradise she was ruined and corrupted in her human nature through Adam, even so upon the tree of the Cross she was redeemed and restored by His giving her the hand of His favour and mercy through His death and passion, and raising the barriers that came from original sin between the soul and God. And this she says, Beneath the Apple-tree. That is, beneath the favour of the Tree of the Cross, which is here understood by the Apple-tree, whereon the Son of God redeemed human nature, and, in consequence betrothed it to Himself, and consequently, betrothed to Himself every soul giving it for this purpose grace and pledges thereof in the Cross.[3]

The language, to be sure, may not appeal to modern ears; but the truth of the soul's redemption by the bearing of our sin in his own body on the tree remains as the unchanging good news of the gospel.

Notes

1. Luther, M., *Works*, ed. Pelikan, J. and Lehmann, H.T., St Louis, Concordia, Philadelphia, Fortress, xxvii, 278f.
2. *ibid.*
3. *The Spiritual Canticle and Poems of St. John of the Cross*, (ed. 1978) tr. Peers, E.Allison, London, Burns & Oates, 312.

Chapter III
THE CUP

In both the Old and New Testament the term 'cup' (Hebrew *kos*, Greek, poterion) denotes primarily a drinking vessel. Its first use appears with this sense in Genesis 40:11 where Joseph dreams of clusters of ripened grapes which he presses into Pharaoh's cup and puts the cup into the monarch's hand. By a metonymy the cup as a container came to signify its contents offered to be drunk. It thus became a common figure to express the experiences of life, be they sweet or bitter. In the religious context the cup became associated with God's appointments and dealings with his people in particular and mankind in general. So, for example, the Psalmist regards God himself as his cup when he sings, 'The Lord is my chosen portion and my cup' (Ps. 16:5). So too does his own cup 'overflow' (Ps. 23:5). But adversity, too, is a 'cup of the Lord's hand' (Hab. 2:16 cf. Ps. 75:8; Jer. 25:17). God's cup may contain judgement on the wicked (cf. Is. 51:17; Jer. 25:15f.; Rev. 14:10; 16:19; 18:6). It can also be a cup of correction for God's own people, to turn them again to the ways of righteousness (cf. Isa. 51:22).

The Passion of our Lord
The most significant use of the term 'cup' in the New Testament is in connection with our Lord's passion. Twice, near the time of the crucifixion, does it come into Christ's own speech; once in a metaphorical sense in his prayer in Gethsemane, and once in a literal sense in the upper room at his institution of the Last Supper. Deeply moving and profoundly significant is our Lord's prayer at the place called Gethsemane: ' "My Father, if it be possible let this cup pass from me; nevertheless, not as I will, but as thou wilt" ' (Matt. 26:39 cf. Mark 14:36; Luke 22:42). The cup from which he prayed to be spared did not involve just the physical pain and suffering of the crucifixion which awaited him.

There must have been in that cup something more deeply felt than pain; something more terrible than reproach; something more unspeakably awful even than the nails in his hands and feet and the sword stabbing his side. There was in that cup given him to drink that which made him 'exceedingly sorrowful and very heavy' in mind, in soul, in spirit, and which caused him to pray in an agony of blood-like sweat that it should pass from him. It was not the fear of coming scorn, nor yet even the dread of public crucifixion, that drove him to utter that prayer. What caused Christ to be sore amazed and troubled in heart was that the cup from which he must drink was held out to him by the hand of his own God and Father. It was his own God and Father who would put him to grief and lay on him the burden of all human iniquity. Not, then, from the Jewish leaders, the Roman authorities, the howling crowd, the traitor Judas, nor yet finally from Satan himself, did the testing now come. Rather was it the case, as C.H. Spurgeon says in a powerful sermon entitled 'The Agony of Gethsemane':

> a cup filled by one He knew to be His Father, but who, nevertheless he understood to have appointed Him a very bitter potion, a cup not to be drunk by His body and to spend its gall upon His flesh, but a cup which specially amazed His soul and troubled His inmost heart. He drank from it, and therefore be ye sure that it was a draught more dreadful than physical pain, since from that he did not shrink; it was a potion more dreadful than reproach, from that he had not turned aside; more dreadful than Satanic temptation, - that he had overcome; it was something inconceivably dreadful, amazingly full of dread which came from the Father's hand.[1]

Both the wrath of God's judgement on sin and the hell of being forsaken by the Father were in the cup. To be under sin's condemnation, to be cut off from communion with God his Father as if himself a sinner, was the real poison in the cup given him to drink. To be wounded for transgressions not his own and bruised for iniquities he did not commit; to be put in the place of death when it belonged to him to have life in himself; to bear in his body humanity's sin when he had no sin of his own to carry; to be under the wrath of God when he before the world's creation was eternally enfolded in the Father's love - such were among the terrible ingredients of the cup which he must drink. To be under the curse of the law on account of sin; to die on a gibbet as one accursed of God - his own God and Father - was for him the most poignant, the most heart-breaking of all. He must take the cup of woe from the Father's hand knowing the bitterness of its potion. All hell was distilled into that cup and he must drink it to the last drop. It was human sin which mixed the ingredients of the cup, and he who knew no sin saw the terrible reality that it is. He alone of the sons of men had the measure of the sin he must take upon himself. He alone knew sin in its every reach and extent, and the absoluteness of God's wrath against it, seeing in the cup all the fullness of sin and the Father's holy judgement of it.

Mark records that with the cross looking dark before him Jesus 'began to be sore amazed' (Mark 14:33 AV). Luther found these words the most astonishing in the whole New Testament. There was nothing in all the world, he declares, that could sore amaze the Son of God but the huge totality of the sin of humanity which must be 'laid on' him. Sin was so exceedingly sinful, so unspeakably evil, that in sore amazement the strong Son of God was pressed down by it to death and hell. None of us really knows what sin is, being ourselves sinners. It belongs to sin itself not to appear as sin. And it belongs to sinners to excuse it, to minimise it, to regard ourselves as not specially evil and our sinful deeds as mere hiccups in our human condition. Of the froth of the cup we may have some little notion; but of the reality itself we know not the first thing. Take away sin's terrible wages, its sure and full discovery and exposure, its first and second death, its day of judgement, and the fire that is not quenched, and see them as mere froth of the cup. Take away all that, and there is left pure, essential, unadulterated sin, what the apostle Paul calls so masterfully, 'the sinfulness of sin' (cf. Rom. 7:13).

As Christ looked into the cup that was proffered to him with all its awful mixture, it is not to be wondered at that he was 'utterly astonished' being 'taken aback' at the dreadful prospect of drinking it. So in 'an agony' he prayed that if it were possible the cup might pass from him. There in Gethsemane a tremendous battle was fought out in the arena of his soul. For as he saw the cup he shrank from the ordeal, yet his pledged obedience and dedication to fulfil the Father's will, not without a struggle, rose triumphantly in him. For there is the note of victory at the end of the prayer, 'nevertheless, not my will but thine be done'. The 'nevertheless' is the recognition that he will most surely carry out to its utmost end the Father's purpose in sending him into the world. It is the 'nevertheless' of acceptance and dedication. 'That was what Jesus did', what 'he attained through the agony of the garden. The agony does not represent a doubt as to his calling against the dreadful temptation to renounce it which came in the hour and with the power of darkness.'[2] So did he accept the cup and drank it all.

Forsaken by God

To bear in himself sin's curse and judgement meant Jesus being forsaken by his God and Father. The awful isolation of the cry of Jesus on the cross, ' "My God, my God, why hast thou forsaken me?" ' (Mark 15:34). cannot be separated in the experience of Christ from some real, if mysterious. connection with the sin he came to deal with in his death on the cross. The sense of God's presence was lost to Christ as he was overwhelmed by the enormity of the cup's awful mixture. There was lost to him - taken from him - that unbroken awareness of the nearness of God his Father which had hitherto been his constant experience. At Calvary God the holy Father who cannot look on sin or behold iniquity dare not lift his eyes on the Son of his love laden with transgressions. He must turn himself away from the terrible scene. For it belongs to sin's nature and being to separate the sinner from God and for God to hide his face from it. So on Calvary's tree did Christ by taking to himself the sin of all sinners, experience the God-forsakenness of sin's judgement. So did God separate himself from him as the scapegoat was sent into the wilderness bearing the sin of the people, away from the presence of God in the sanctuary. Writes Eberhard Jungel, 'That this man dies for *us*, that he became a curse *for us* on the gallows, can be asserted only on the basis of an event which interprets the God-forsakenness of his death *positively*.[3] Hanged on a tree, by the law accursed, Jesus exclaimed on the cross, "My God, my God, why hast thou forsaken me?", and yet at the end he can say, ' "Father into thy hands I commit my spirit" ' (Luke 23:46). God who had turned his back on his Son made 'a curse' and 'sin' for us, turned to him again as he declared finished the work he came to do at the Father's bidding.

Therefore, says Jungel,

Because he depended totally on God, he not only initiated this conflict of the law (that would condemn him as one accursed) with itself, but he submitted himself to this conflict which then ended in God-forsakenness. By depending totally on God his life ended in the event of God-forsakenness. The special severity of Jesus' God-forsakenness on the cross, is the experience of that God-forsakenness by an existence derived solely from God. The Marcan cry of the dying Christ, interpreted with Psalm 22:1, can express that God-forsakenness as vividly as it does only because its precondition is God-relatedness. Jesus' fatal God-forsakenness is not lessened by that, but rather intensified to an extreme degree because it occurs within the context of a unique certainty of God. The God whose coming was proclaimed by Jesus has now forsaken him on the cross. That Jesus, according to Mark, cries out to the God who is forsaking him, ' "My God, my God, why has thou forsaken me?" ' (Mark 15:34), is the experience of a distance of God which is not his fault, which was caused by the law, and which exceeds the hell of godlessness in that Jesus' lifelong insistence on the coming of God is compressed into this cry. Paul's interpretation is harsh, but precise; he became a 'curse' (Gal. 3:13).[4]

In Christ's God-forsakenness on the cross, we are, then, in touch with the ultimate mystery of the divine transaction for the open possibility of man's redemption which lies in the final mystery of the Godhead. Calvin regards the God-forsakenness of Christ as giving meaning to the credal statement, 'he descended into hell'. He thus asserts that,

Nothing had been done if Christ had only endured corporeal death. In order to interpose between us and God's anger and satisfy his righteous judgement, it was necessary that he should feel the weight of divine vengeance. Whence also it was necessary that he engage, as it were, at close quarters with the powers of hell and the horror of eternal death.[5]

This is, indeed, a strong statement and one which even some Reformed theologians hesitate to support. Nevertheless, there was for Christ in the cup he would drink the terrible awareness of God-forsakenness so that in some sense he was sharing in and taking to himself the reality of sin as resulting in banishment from God's presence and fellowship. In the agony of the garden he accepted that in his death he would be burdened by the world's sin, and being thus numbered with transgressors in the sin-bearing event of Calvary, he must of necessity experience the desolation of God-forsakenness. Thus does Christ take the cup that the Father had given him to drink (John 18:11) and, betrayed by Judas and falsely condemned by the rulers, go to Calvary's cross to die for our sins (1 Cor. 15:3), the just for the unjust, to bring us to God (1 Pet. 3:18).

It is because of his drinking the cup of our sins' judgement that there is now no condemnation for such as are in Christ Jesus (Rom. 8:1). It is because of his forsakenness by God in the bearing of the curse of human sin as separation from God that our access (Eph. 2:18) to God is achieved. Thus does the cup of suffering become the cup of redemption for all who 'take the cup of salvation and call upon the name of the Lord' (Ps. 116:13 AV). For that literal cup of the outpoured wine is eloquent in its symbolism of the cup proclaiming his blood shed for many for the remission of sins. In the cross the symbolic cup of Gethsemane was made actual; and the actual cup of the upper room became symbolic. For through Christ's death the symbolic cup had its actualisation as atonement and the actual cup received its symbolisation as redemption. So was the cup of the wrath of God in sin's judgement merged in the cup of God's love for sin's forgiveness. Such is the cup of the new covenant in Christ's blood (1 Cor. 11:25), and 'the cup of blessing which we bless' (1 Cor. 10:16). The cup which Jesus passed round to his disciples corresponds to that which in the paschal ritual bore the name of *kos*, the cup of blessing which the father of the family circulated to close the feast. The use of the definite article - *to*,' the', - designates the cup specifically as the one which stood there before him, i.e. Jesus at the last supper. But it is now given a new significance to typify the blood shed for the remission of sins through which men and women are brought together into the family of God, and the blood of the covenant to ratify his promises of faithfulness to his redeemed people.

Notes

1. Spurgeon, C.H., *Twelve Sermons on the Passion and Death of Christ*, London, Passmore & Alabastor, 43f.
2. Denney, James, (1911) *The Death of Christ*, (rev. edn), London. Hodder & Stoughton, 45.
3. Jungel, Eberhard, *God as the Mystery of the World*, tr. (1983) Guder, Darrel L., Edinburgh, T. & T. Clark, 361.
4. *ibid*.
5. Calvin, J., *The Institutes of the Christian Religion*, tr. (1949) Beveridge, Henry, Cambridge, James Clarke, 11, XVI, 10.

Chapter IV
THE DEATH

Several other words and phrases in the New Testament focus attention on the significance of Christ's death. These various synonyms emphasise both the actuality of Christ's work as a historical fact and its reality as saving truth. Of these 'crucified' and 'slain' are chief in importance. The historical fact is that 'they crucified him' (Matt. 27:35 AV). But for Paul the apostle that historical fact seen from the standpoint of the gospel given to him by revelation, (cf. Gal. 1:11), is the essential means of man's salvation. He thus affirms it to be his one object and burden to 'preach Christ crucified' (1 Cor. 1:23). So Eberhard Jungel rightly declares, 'The theology of the Crucified One answers the question about the content and origin of the Christian faith.'[1] That Christ was slain is, too, a historical fact: him 'they slew and hanged on a tree' (Acts 10:39 AV). Yet in that fact of the slain Christ the redeemed of the Lord rejoice. It was by his being slain, that by 'his blood' he did 'ransom men for God from every tribe and tongue and people and nation' (Rev. 5:9).

It is, however, on the words 'death' and 'die' in connection with the work of Christ that the emphasis falls in the New Testament. Christ was aware that 'to die' was his destiny. He knew himself as the son cast out of the vineyard and killed (Matt. 21:38-39). And following on Peter's confession of his messiahship and his divine sonship (Matt. 16:16), he told his disciples that he must be 'killed' in Jerusalem (Matt. 16:21). When he told his disciples that when a grain of wheat falls into the ground and dies, 'it bears much fruit' (John 12:24), Christ was not merely giving them a lesson on the need for ultimate self-sacrifice on their part - although without doubt that lesson was plainly there to be learned. Rather, there was in his words an allusion to his own full sacrifice unto death. The words recorded later in the chapter apply here, too: 'He said this to show by what death he was to die' (v. 33). That Jesus himself accepted the inevitability of his death and consequently, therefore, its necessity for the work of God he had come to fulfil is a fact so evident from the Gospels as to be beyond the least doubt. And he did die on a Roman gibbet. He was crucified, slain, killed - all these words are used of the deed done by the Roman authorities and the Jewish leaders on Golgotha's hill. But the most apposite and the most significant word of all is that he 'died'. To be crucified, to be slain, to be killed, is to have one's life taken away by others. But to die is something one does, so to speak, for oneself. Christ was crucified, slain, killed at the hands of wicked men. But he also died, brought himself to die - for it was with him not to die. He laid down his life of himself (John 10:17, 18) as a matter of his own choosing, in obedience to his Father's will. He 'gave himself' to the death of the cross. He buried himself as the 'seed' in the soil of human existence to die that he might bring forth much fruit. His death is to be read in terms of a sacrificial atonement for human sin and the means of man's redemption to God.

All the writers of the New Testament refer to Christ's death as effecting man's salvation to its fullest measure. Paul's statement in 1 Corinthians 15:3, 'I delivered to you as of first importance what I also received, that Christ died for our sins in accordance with the scriptures', emphasised the fact that the death of Christ has a specific cause-effect connection with God's forgiveness of sin. Commenting on this verse Smeaton says, 'The words, beyond doubt, refer to our sins as the meritorious cause of Christ's death; and the thought expressed is that the death of Christ was a punishment of sin.'[2] It is this significance of the death of Christ in relation to sin that must be carried through into its several occurrences in the New Testament. But Paul's words suggest that this featuring of Christ's death as 'of first importance' is not only the gospel divinely communicated to him, but also the essential focus of Old Testament prophecy (cf. Luke 24:44-49). Understandable, then, is the apostolic preoccupation with the Calvary event.

Paul may, however, be considered the theologian, *par excellence*, of the death of Christ, as he in particular seeks to give significance to Christ's work under that term. (The several references in the Epistle to the Hebrews to Christ's death are stated by contrast with the ancient Levitical ritual to highlight the superiority of the new way of salvation through the sacrificial death of Jesus). Paul's doctrine of the death of Christ is concerned less with the historical details than with its atoning efficacy for the redemption of mankind. Paul's approach to the Calvary event was not primarily from the perspective of the crucifixion - what men did to Christ as the expression of human sin. His approach was from the cross itself - what God did in Christ for the expiation of human sin. By Christ's obedience unto death, 'even the death of the cross' (Phil 2:8 AV) Paul is sure, as he is anxious to declare, that 'we were reconciled to God' (Rom. 5:10). Thus is Paul's theology of the death of Christ explicit. Had not Christ died for us we would still be in our sins and under the wrath of God. This was the apostle's one message on Christ's death from first to last of his Christian career.[3] While in virtually all his letters Paul in some way refers to the death of Christ, it is in his letter to the Romans that the expressions 'Christ died' or 'his death' occur more frequently than in all the others put together. He states that 'Christ died for the ungodly' (5:6); that 'while we were yet sinners Christ died for us' (v. 8); that 'while we were enemies we were reconciled to God by the death of his son' (v. 10). He 'died to sin once for all' (6:10); 'it is Christ Jesus who died, yes, who was raised from the dead' (8:34), he proclaims. And being baptised 'into his death' (6:3), we are 'united with him in a death like his' (6:5). As baptism focuses on the fact of 'his death', so, too, does the communion service celebrate 'the Lord's death until he comes' (1 Cor. 11:26). In the body of his flesh through death Christ has reconciled all things to himself (Col. 1:20).

Such are the data from which Paul's theology of the death of Christ is to be framed. In that death there is provided for sinners an objective atonement which secures the sinner's reconciliation to God and his restoration to fellowship with him. So is Christ's death truly a 'sacrifice of atonement'. For the ungodly, for sinners, for enemies, Christ died. Through his death the ungodly have divine righteousness, sinners divine remission and enemies divine reconciliation.

Paul's gospel, then centres on the death of Christ. And he proclaimed that gospel of the death of Christ, not as a means to move the human soul to the response of compassion, but as the ground upon which man may be justified in the sight of God and saved from the wrath to come (Rom. 5:9). The atoning efficacy of Christ's work is powerfully attested in Paul's designation of a Christian as 'one for whom Christ died' (Rom. 14:15). If, then, it be enquired what did Christ do in the Calvary event for man's sin, Paul's answer is quite definite: 'he died for sin'. Even more personally he would say: 'he died for us'. And then he would specifically individualise it as his own testimony: 'he loved me, and gave himself [he died] for me' (Gal. 2:20).

Necessity

It is in the atonement of the death of Christ that God's honour. justice and wrath have their fullest expression and their final satisfaction. If, then, there is forgiveness with God at all, it is realised solely on the grounds of Christ's death. But it is out of his love that the sacrifice of Christ's atonement has its ultimate cause and its final goal. God is, indeed, a God of holiness with whom sin cannot dwell, yet he is a God of love who would have man reconciled to himself. Therefore, if God in his love would establish a relationship with man, sin in its every manifestation had to be dealt with by its removal as a barrier to the process by which God would mediate his forgiveness. Only in the atoning actuality of the death of Christ, in which God's holy judgement on sin had its completest satisfaction. can the fullness of God's love be realised. 'The Divine Love is known in the greatness of the resistance which it overcomes.'[4] The use of the term 'satisfaction' in this connection is,

> an appropriate word, providing we realise that it is he [God] himself in his inner being who needs to be satisfied, and not something external to himself. Talk of law, honour, justice, the moral order is true in so far as they are seen as expressions of God's character. Atonement is a 'necessity' because it 'arises from within God himself.'[5]

The necessity of the atonement lies deep in the nature of God and his relation to man. Such is the 'must' of Christ's death: 'The Son of man must suffer many things ... and be killed' (Mark 8:31; cf. Luke 17:25). For, as Athanasius says, 'death there had to be, and death for all, that the due of all might be paid.'[6] And again, elsewhere, 'Christ endured death for us inasmuch as he offered himself for the purpose of God.'[7]

But if in Christ's death there is atonement for sin, there was there, too, the acceptance by Christ of sin's wages as death in order to abolish death itself and bring 'life and immortality to light through the gospel' (2 Tim. 1:10). Christ's death was not only an atonement for sin's reality. it was also the cancellation of death as sins's wages. For Athanasius, 'The death of the incarnate Logos is a ransom for the sins of man, and the death of death.'[8] The phrase the 'death of death' was later to become enshrined in the title of John Owen's famous volume on the atonement, *The Death of Death in the Death of Christ* (1647), in which he declares,

> the death of Christ made satisfaction in the very thing that was required in the obligation. He took away the curse, by 'being made a curse' (Gal. 3:13). He delivered us from sin, being 'made sin' (2 Cor. 5:21). He underwent death, that he might deliver us from death.[9]

He partook of human flesh and blood, says the writer of the Epistle to the Hebrews, 'that through death he might destroy him who has the power of death, that is, the devil' (Heb. 2:14).

The first and worst result of death which is the 'wages of sin' (Rom. 6:23) is man's separation from God. Sin came into the world through one man, and death through sin, and so death 'spread to all men because all men sinned' (Rom. 5:12). Death is the dread sentence pronounced by God on man for the sinner that he is. But Christ in his death took to himself this punitive relation between sin and death. By putting away sin by the sacrifice of himself Jesus by his death abolished death as separation from God, to restore man to God as the source of life (Rom. 4:17) and immortality (1 Tim. 6:16).

'Sin reigns in death' (Rom. 5:21), but Christ in his death has conquered sin, so that death has been 'abolished' in his victory. It is sin that takes the central place among the powers that hold man in slavery, while all the powers of evil stand in relation to this terrible reality. Allied to sin is death; but in his defeat of sin Christ has destroyed death's dominion over man. Sin and death are related to the devil as the source of their power. From that power Christ has delivered man in the vicarious and victorious act of his death. Not only in that Calvary event is sin annulled and death abolished, but 'the reason the Son of God appeared was to destroy the works of the devil' (1 John 3:8), and to render void his power until his final destruction at the end time (cf. Rev. 12:9,12; 20:2,10). Thus with the cross as his destiny rising before him Christ declares, ' " I saw Satan fall like lightning from heaven" ' (Luke 10:18). In the death of Christ all the armed forces of evil were conquered: sin as the power of death, death as the power of the devil and the devil as the power of sin and death. In the victory of Christ in the death of the cross, sin has been robbed of its strength, death has been deprived of its sting and the devil stripped of his dominion. The catalogue of all that was charged against sinners by the open hostility of the united trio of sin, death and the devil, Christ has taken away, nailing it to his cross. Christ has already won the victory over all evil in the Calvary event.

The triumph of Christ over sin, death and the devil is not only a victory to be won *within* us which in imperfect measure reflects and repeats that of Gethsemane's garden and Golgotha's cross, but it is also a victory won for us, in a sphere outside and beyond our experience, yet essential for the full divine redemption into which we are initiated by faith.

In faith believers, in their total spiritual and psychical selfhood, answer the atoning Christ; and discover in their answering that in the atonement of the death of Christ they have been found by Christ. It is Christ's death as a historical fact in which Christ stood in for us that alters everything infinitely in God's relation to us. For Christ, in his death, has triumphed over everything evil that would stand between us and God, so that God can move towards us in the fullness of his grace in forgiveness. Such is the good news of the gospel: that the Christ who was not under condemnation for sins of his own entered into death (Phil. 2:8; 1 Cor. 5:7; 1 Pet. 3:18); and by dying 'for us' (Mark 10:45, Rom. 5:6; 1 Thess. 5:10; Heb. 2:9) he took himself our death as sin's deserved judgement. James Denney puts it,

> The atonement, as the New Testament presents it, assumes a connection of sin and death. Apart from some sense and recognition of such connection, the mediation of forgiveness through the death of Christ can only appear an arbitrary, irrational, unacceptable idea.[10]

Sin and Death

The biblical revelation does certainly connect sin and death. It declares a cause-effect relation between them. At the beginning of history this connection and relation is affirmed by God himself to the parents of the human family in his warning against transgressing his divine command, ' "In the day you eat of it you shall die" ' (Gen. 2:17). Because of Adam's sinning, the spiritual death of separation from God and the physical death as the cessation of natural life passed unto all men, for all have sinned.

Man was not created as 'not able to die', for such immortality belongs to God alone. But it was open to man to maintain the condition of being 'able not to die'. But he did not. He sinned. And as a result of his fall death became his common lot with the whole of the natural creation. Since man exists as one being in a twofold relation to the spiritual and natural - he is of God and of the ground - the death to which he became subject is, consequently, likewise a duality at once spiritual and natural. The biblical writers are at one in presenting man in the full integrity of his being, and in relation to God. They do not sever the distinction between the spiritual, moral and natural - physical which has, in fact, no meaning for God in his relation to man. They were aware of, and sensitive to, the unity of the human person. One great instance of the oneness of the spiritual and the natural is the unity of sin and death. In death the spiritual and the natural reach the vanishing point of their distinction.

As, therefore, sin and death affect man in the duality of his one person, so does the death of Christ for man's salvation redeem him in the unity of his need by reason of his sin and death. So was Christ's death at once spiritual, a separation from God; and physical, he bore our sins in his body to the tree. 'Sin involved man in death, and Christ could not deal effectively, except he took the consequences upon himself.'[11] There is thus a punitive relation between sin and death; he died for our sins and abolished death. In his death he took from death its sting (1 Cor. 15:55-56). In his death he abolished on our behalf spiritual death - the death of the soul's separation from God. And in his death he transformed physical death from an awesome terror to a welcome guest. Thus does Paul see death as a conquered enemy (1 Cor. 15:26); the one last enemy to be met and mastered by the life-giving death of Christ. As a man 'alive again' in Christ, Paul was sure that death had been vanquished in the cross of Calvary (2 Tim. 1:10). Jesus Christ has robbed sin of its power: and in his death, death itself, in its every expression, physical, spiritual and eternal has its measure and mastery. And life, the life that is in Christ Jesus, is open to all who would pluck the healing leaves from the tree of life on Golgotha's hill. Emil Brunner is right: 'That a death - this most hideous dreadful death - must redeem, and has redeemed us. this is the non-modern, anti-modern Gospel of the Bible.'[12]

Notes

1. Jungel, E., *God as the Mystery of the World*; tr. (1983) Guder, Edinburgh, T. & T. Clark, 362.
2. Smeaton, George, (1957) *The Apostles' Doctrine of the Atonement*, Grand Rapids, Zondervan, 207.
3. Denney, J.,(1911)*The Death of Christ*, (rev. edn) London, Hodder & Stoughton, 83.
4. Brunner, E., (1934) *The Mediator*, tr, Wyon O., London, Lutterworth, 468.
5. Stott, John, *The Cross of Christ*, Leicester, Inter-Varsity Press, 123. Wallace, Ronald S. (1981) *The Atoning Death of Christ*, London, Marshall. Morgan & Scott, 113.
6. Athanasius, *De Incarnatione*, iv, 20.
7. Athanasius, *Against the Arians* i, 41.
8. *ibid.*, i, 45.
9. Owen, John, *The Death of Death in the Death of Christ*, ed. (1959) Goold, William H., London, Banner of Truth, 156.
10. Denney, *op. cit.*, 291.
11. Jeweth, P.J., (1975) 'Death', in Tenney, Merril C. (ed.), *Zondervan Pictorial Encyclopedia of the Bible*, Grand Rapids, Zondervan, ii, 77.
12. Brunner, *op. cit.*, 54.

Chapter V
THE BLOOD

More perhaps even than the phrase 'the cross' that of 'the blood' encapsulates all that the New Testament signifies by the Calvary event. Not only is the cost of redemption present in the word itself, but also its content. It is in the actuality of the shed blood of Christ that all that pertains to man's salvation has its cause and condition. It is not, therefore, surprising that the apostle Peter should speak of it as 'the precious blood of Christ' (1 Pet. 1:19). Even in the old economy, which was a shadow of the better things to come, God never dealt with sin without blood (cf. Heb. 9:22). There was no remission without the blood of sacrifice. No remission was proffered or pronounced on the strength of a deep repentance or a future emendation which was not linked with the outpouring of blood. Spices or incense, money or meal were of no avail without its shedding. It was because of the blood that the people of Israel were permitted to enter the courts of the Lord to worship. Because of the blood they had access to the sanctuary of God. The blood was thus for them the at-one-ment; the way of their reconciliation to, and acceptance by, God. Such was the truth written deeply into the sacrificial ritual of the Levitical code, in which was shadowed forth the gospel truth that 'being now justified by his [Christ's] blood, we shall be saved from wrath through him' (Rom. 5:9 AV).

All the New Testament letter with the exception of the lesser epistles to Philemon and of James: those of Paul, Peter, John and the writer of the Epistle to the Hebrews, focus heavily on 'the blood shed' as the alpha and omega of God's scheme for the salvation of sinners. Each synoptic writer records our Lord's words at the institution of the Last Supper. 'this is my blood of the new covenant which is poured out for many for the remission of sins' (Matt. 26:28; Mark 14:24; Luke 22:20; cf. Acts 20:28). And that blood was neither for Christ himself, nor for his apostles as interpreters of the Calvary event, a mere symbol of a dedicated life or yet or a self-sacrificing act for men of good will to copy. For Christ did not shed his blood as an example for the righteous to follow but as a sacrifice for sinners to embrace. The blood of Christ is the means of their justification (Rom. 5:9); the method of their redemption (Eph. 1:7; cf. 1 Pet. 1:19); the sphere of their peace (Col. 1:20); the way of their acceptance (Eph. 2:13; cf. 1:6); the assurance of their access (Heb. 10:19; cf. Rom. 5:2; Eph. 3:12): the vehicle of their cleansing (1 John 1:7; cf. Rev. 1:5); the power of their sanctification (Heb. 13:12; cf. 2:11; 9:13; Eph. 5:26; 1 Thess. 5:23; 1 Pet. 3:15); and the energy of their victory (Rev. 12:11;cf. 1 Cor. 15:27; John 16:33; 1 John 4:4).

The passages in the Gospels - Matthew 26:28; Mark 14:24; Luke 22:20 (AV); John 6:53-55, - in which 'the blood of Christ' has a specific redemptive meaning must be taken in conjunction with those statements in the epistles about 'the blood of Christ' (1 Cor. 10:16; Eph. 2:13; Heb. 9:14); 'the blood of the Lord' (1 Cor. 11:27); 'the blood of the cross' (Col. 1:20); 'the blood of Jesus' (1 John 1:7); 'the blood of Jesus Christ' (1 Pet. 1:2); and 'the blood of the Lamb' (Rev. 12:11). In all these passages the 'preciousness' of the blood, as the apostle speaks of it (1 Pet. 1:19) is understood in relation to its subject. The blood is precious because of who he was that gave himself for its shedding. It was the blood of Christ, the Lord, the Lamb of God. C.H. Spurgeon in a remarkable sermon on 1 Peter 1:19 eloquently extols the 'preciousness' of the blood shed for man's salvation. He says,

'the blood of Christ' - here powers of speech would fail to convey to you an idea of its preciousness. Behold here, a person innocent, without taint within, or flaw without, a person meritorious, who magnified the law and made it honourable - a person who served both God and man even unto death. Nay, here you have a divine person, - so divine that in the Acts of the Apostles Paul calls his blood the 'blood of God'. Place innocence, and merit, and dignity, and position and Godhead itself, in the scale and then conceive what must be the inestimable value of the blood which Jesus poured forth.

Spurgeon goes on in the sermon to speak of the 'usefulness' of the blood to the people of God; and ends with a plea to his hearers to 'turn those eyes of yours to the full atonement made, to the utmost ransom paid'.[1]

Clearly, for Spurgeon to speak of the blood of Christ was at one with proclaiming the death of Christ. For him it was certainly the true reading of the New Testament to take the phrase 'the blood of Christ' in connection with the work of Christ to mean nothing other than Christ's actual death on the cross. Spurgeon would not have deemed it a right interpretation of the Calvary event to regard the phrase 'the blood of Christ' as meaning the releasing of Christ's dedicated life rather than signifying the efficacy of his sacrificial death. For, as in the case of the term 'the cross of Christ', 'the blood of Christ' is another way of declaring that the actual death of Christ has redemptive meaning and atoning significance.

Life released

By a strange quirk of eccentric exegesis, which came into fashion during the last decade of the nineteenth century, 'the blood of Christ' came to be interpreted not as referring to Christ's death for our redemption but as a releasing of his life for our enlightenment. The idea seems to have been first advanced in Germany by C. Bahr in his *Symbolk des Mosaischen Cultus* (1874). He proclaimed the dictum, 'Blood atones by means of the life that is in it'. This interpretation of the phrase 'the blood' was introduced to the English speaking world by H.C. Trumbull. Following Bahr, Trumbull bases his contention on Leviticus 17:14, 'For the life of every creature is the blood of it', and Deuteronomy 12:23, 'the blood is the life'. It is argued in the light of these declarations that the blood in connection with the symbolic sacrifices of the earlier economy is to be understood as the outflow of the life principle which constitutes an atonement for the soul (cf. Lev. 17:11). Trumbull explains: 'It was not the death of the victim, nor yet the broken body; but it was the blood, the soul, that was made the means of the soul's ransom, of its rescue, of its redemption.'[2] Connecting this idea with the work of Christ, Trumbull then interprets:

> Having in his own blood the life of God and the life of man, Jesus Christ would make men sharers of the Divine by making them sharers of his own nature, and this was the truth of truths which he declared to those whom he instructed.[3]

In the subsequent period this interpretation of the blood of Christ gained widespread approval. Thus, for example, C.A. Beckwith in an article on the phrase in Hastings' *Dictionary of the Apostolic Church* and W.O.E. Osterley in his article on the same subject in *The Dictionary of Christ and the Gospels* assert that no other interpretation is either credible or valid. So Beckwith comments:

> For the blood represents the life, even if this is taken by violence. Christ's blood freely given, with the sole aim of recovering men in sin to fellowship with God, and to their Divine destination as children of God. The efficacy of the life of Christ thus given is continuous from the unseen world and in the purpose of God. Thus the blood which flowed once for all is not of transitory worth, but is endowed with the energy perpetually to create new redemptive personal and social values - It is eternal.[4]

Among the theologians and commentators who adopt this view that the blood stands, not for the reality of Christ's death, but for the release to universal energy of his life, are Vincent Taylor and C.H. Dodd. Both of these writers in turn are indebted to B.F. Westcott as their mentor. In two added notes on 'The Blood', one in his *Commentary on the Epistles of St John*, and the other in his *Commentary on Hebrews*, Westcott sought to give a show of plausibility to the interpretation. Declaring that 'the blood is the life', Westcott argues, that in Christ's physical death, the 'principle of life' was 'liberated' to become 'available for others'. The blood poured forth is the same with the shedding abroad of the living energy of Christ's life for the impartation of divine life to man. Holding this interpretation, it is only to be expected that Westcott should emphatically reject the substitutionary doctrine of Christ's death. He consequently asserts, in spite of those passages of scripture which categorically declare the fact and others that definitely imply it, that the substitutionary penal view regarding the work of the Calvary event has no biblical support.[5] He therefore says, regarding the work of Christ:

it is enough for us to remember that Christ fulfilled the words which he spoke to his disciples in the accomplishment of his own work, and that he has brought the power of sacrifice as a revelation of a larger life, of victorious influences, of an eternal blessing, within the reach of the humblest believer who claims the virtue of his blood,[6]

or, to substitute for the last word, what is his actual view, the value of his [Christ's] life.

It is supposed that, by interpreting the phrase 'the blood of Christ' in terms of the release of his divine life, these writers are merely assaying a modern statement of the divinisation of the human individual by the actuality of Christ's work proposed by Irenaeus and Athanasius. There are, indeed, passages in the works of both Irenaeus and Athanasius to support the thesis. Both advance the idea that by his work Christ has restored to man his immortality by the infusion of his own divine life. Says Irenaeus:

For no other means could we have obtained to incorruption and immortality, unless we had been united in incorruptibility and immortality. But how could we be joined to incorruption and immortality, unless first incorruptibility and immortality had become what we are, so that the corruptible might be swallowed up by incorruptibility, and the mortal by immortality, that we might receive the adoption of sons?[7]

Words of similar import may be quoted from Athanasius. But the two views; that proposed by Trumbull and Westcott, and that suggested by Irenaeus and Athanasius, are in the end by no means akin. For on the crucial issue of the locale of the life-imparting efficacy of the work of Christ they are specifically different. For, while Trumbull and Westcott speak of the divinising energy of Christ's life enshrined in the concept of his blood, as *life* released, Irenaeus and Athanasius both see man's resultant deification as grounded in the atoning efficacy of his actual *death*. Irenaeus is quite explicit, 'Christ did suffer, and was himself the Son of God who died for us, and redeemed us with his blood'[8]. And, says Athanasius, 'The Lord offered for our sakes the one death,'[9] and, 'Christ endured death for us.'[10]

Life laid down

On the face of it, it seems incredible that anyone should conceive of the shedding of Christ's blood as the releasing of his divine life for man's deification rather than his death for man's salvation. In view of the number of references to Christ's suffering, cross and the pouring forth and laying down of his life, it would seem impossible to take the shedding of his blood as other than a reference to his death. Nothing would appear more certain than that the New Testament itself intends the phrase to be so read. Indeed, it looks as if Paul would forestall the contrary notion when in Romans 5:9-10 he uses the terms 'the blood' and 'the death' of Christ in parallel, where the latter clearly establishes the meaning of the former. So to speak of 'the blood of Christ' is at one with speaking of 'the death of Christ'. Thus R.K. Harrison is right to affirm,

> The sacrificial blood is associated with the death of the Saviour (Heb. 9:14), and the author of Hebrews makes it plain that the blood is associated with death rather than life (Heb. 12:24). It seems evident, therefore, that sacrifices were efficacious through the death of the victim, and the blood indicates life given up in death not life set free.[11]

In recent years a number of studies have been published which show that what we may call the 'blood-life' view cannot be maintained. It is demonstrated beyond dispute that in the cases of the shedding of the blood of sacrifice in the Old Testament economy its efficacious virtue is specifically in the victim's death. Consistent with this fact, therefore, it must be granted that the phrase 'the blood of Christ' is to be understood as signifying his atoning death. John Stott draws attention to Alan Stibbs' excellent Tyndale monograph, *The Meaning of the Word 'Blood' in Scripture*, in which, after an intensive study of its many usages (some 362 in the Old Testament) he concludes that, even in those passages which link 'blood' with 'life', and the 'blood shed' with the 'life outpoured', blood stands 'not for the release of life from the burden of the flesh, but for the bringing to an end of life in the flesh. It is a witness to physical death, not an evidence of spiritual survival.'[12] An equally strong statement is made by Leon Morris. For Morris the witness of scripture is clear. Only by a particular interpretation of a few passages can a case be made for thinking that the blood means life. When the evidence is viewed as a whole, Morris declares, it is beyond reasonable doubt that the 'blood' stands not for life set free, but a life given up in death.

There are 93 occurrences of the term 'blood' (*haima*) in the New Testament, apart from two other special terms used (Matt. 9:20; Heb. 9:22). The greater number of these are in Hebrews (20) and in Revelation (17). Of the 20 usages in Hebrews, 12 refer to the blood of animals (cf. Heb. 9:7,

12,13 etc.) all of which point to the victim's death and, therefore, by analogy make it crystal clear that the blood of Christ refers to the death of Christ as a sacrifice enacted for man's salvation. For the writer of Hebrews the meaning of the phrase 'the blood' is derived by reference to its sacrificial significance in the Old Testament, which in a very inadequate manner prefigured the offering Christ made of himself to the death on the cross for our redemption. In Hebrews 9:14 Christ's sacrificial blood is clearly associated with his death as having saving purport. And in every other instance of its use 'the blood of Christ' is connected with his saving work. In Hebrews 9:7f. the blood of sacrifice, associated with the Day of Atonement, is seen to prefigure Christ, who by his own blood brought to an end the alienation of humanity from God, and of God from sinful mankind. The 'blood of Christ' is at once a sign of Christ's voluntary giving of himself and a statement of the atoning efficacy of his death (cf. Heb. 9:12-14). By the blood of the cross the covenant of our forgiveness is ratified and sealed (Matt. 26:28; cf. Ex. 24:6-8; 1 Cor. 11:25; Heb. 9:15 - 20; 13:20). The blood of Christ denotes the purchase price of our deliverance from sin (cf. Acts 20:28; Eph. 1:7; 1 Pet. 1:19), and the propitiatory sacrifice for the remission of sin (Rom. 3:25; 5:9; Heb. 9:12). The book of Revelation is likewise dominated by the Old Testament use of the term 'blood' and, although it is in large measure influenced by apocalyptic language, the common note of redemption through the blood of Christ is heard throughout (cf. Rev. 1:5; 5:9). When, then, we speak of the blood of Christ, we use an expression for his work as mediating the salvation of God which no other phrase can so well express. Christ by his blood did something once for all for us in the Calvary event. By his blood he broke the bond of sin's hold upon us and brought us into such a relationship with God that we, as his children, can speak to him as, 'Abba, Father'.

Notes

1. Spurgeon, C.H., (1975) *Twelve Sermons on the Passion and Death of Christ*, Grand Rapids, Eerdmans, 33-34. Quoted also in the author's 'The Atonement of the Death of Christ', 21.
2. Trumbull, H.C., (1886) *The Blood Covenant*, London, 286; cf. his (1895) *Studies in Oriental Social Life*, London, 157ff.
3. Trumbull, *The Blood Covenant*, 274.
4. Beckwith, C.A., (1915) article in Hastings, James (ed.) *Dictionary of the Apostolic Church*, Edinburgh, T. & T. Clark, i, 54.
5. Westcott, B.F., (1888) *The Victory of the Cross, Sermons Preached During Holy Week, 1888, in Hereford Cathedral*, London, MacMillan, 79.
6. *ibid.*, 34-35.

7. Irenaeus, *Adversus Haeresus*, iii, 19, 1.
8. *ibid.*, iii, 16, 9.
9. Athanasius, *De Incarnatione*, iv, 25.
10. Athanasius, *Against the Arians*, i, 41.
11. Harrison, R.K., (1975) 'Blood', in Tenney, Merril C. (ed.) *Zondervan Pictorial Encyclopaedia of the Bible*, i, 627.
12. Stott, John, *The Cross of Christ*, Leicester, Inter-Varsity Press, 160; Stibbs, Alan *The Meaning of the term 'Blood' in the New Testament*, London, Tyndale Press, 16.

Chapter VI
THE BODY

Every time the Communion Supper is celebrated, of which the breaking of bread is an integral part, that act is usually accomplished by a repeating of Christ's words,' "This is my body, broken for you" ' (1 Cor.11:24 AV). Those words have in themselves, as has the symbolic act itself, a significance as uniting the person and work of Christ in the redemptive purpose of the Calvary event. The words 'my body' have a Christological import as marking the true humanness of the one who came to bring about for man the salvation of God; while the affirmation 'my body broken for you' has soteriological significance as declaring the way and cost by which that salvation has been secured.

True Humanity
Christ's reference to his 'body' is his own emphatic assertion of his authentic humanness, and so gives reality and integrity to his incarnation as the Word of God made flesh. This is 'my body', declared Jesus, taking the symbolic bread in his hands; the body of the 'me', of Jesus the Christ. For while the 'me' is not to be identified with the body, yet there is still no reality of the 'me' without the body. It is as a body that the 'me' has empirical actuality and locates a person in history, and gives an individual a name and a place.[1] Only in a body subject to space-time conditions can a human person be known and his attitudes and actions be affirmed and assessed. It was thus only in terms of manhood, in his presence as a human body, that the Son of God could accomplish for humanity the divine necessity for its salvation in his 'body broken for you'.

It is thus that Christian faith declares for the full humanness of Jesus and maintains against all who, for whatever reason, would dissolve Christ's personhood into an unreality. It insists that Jesus was a real man subject to our human conditions. The apostolic church set its face against the Docetae who questioned the reality of Christ's humanness, and the post-apostolic church had to insist, against the Laodicaean bishop Apollinarius, upon the full integrity of Christ's person. The Docetae viewed the body of Christ as an illusion and the Apollinarians reduced the body of Christ to an incompleteness. But an illusory Jesus or an incomplete Christ does not meet the requirements of gospel faith. For this reason the First Epistle of John was written to show the necessity of the full humanity of Jesus for faith (1 John 1:1; 2:11; 4:2-3); and the Epistle to the Hebrews to insist upon the necessity of the full humanity of Jesus for salvation (Heb. 2:14f.).

To redeem man, God must reveal himself in terms of our common experience and on the plane of human history. The human reality of Jesus is the historic implication and living vindication of this necessity. Therefore was it prophesied (cf. Ps. 40:6-9), and, therefore, in his coming was it declared that God 'prepared' for him a body (Heb. 10:5). The purpose of the Son of God taking to himself a body was to enable him to do the will of God and to give his life as a sacrifice for sin. In human flesh, he came to accomplish for man a salvation which required that he give himself to the death of the cross. Thus the Jesus presented to us in the four Gospels, and interpreted to us in the rest of the New Testament, was no unearthly angelic visitant, no demigod in human shape. He was a real man who lived his life amid the human realities of our common way. It was as man Jesus came, lived and died. In the Epistle to the Hebrews Christ's full humanness is given special significance in the fulfilment of his redeeming work. The writer is well acquainted with the historical Jesus who lived and suffered. In consequence of his earthly experience he grew in wisdom and stature and in favour with God and man. For he did not come upon earth as a fully fashioned Saviour. He had, so to speak, to make experience of our human ways and work himself into his place for the fulfilment of his Father's will for the redemption of mankind.

Among early Church writers, Tertullian laid heavy emphasis on the necessity of Christ's humanness for the enactment of man's redemption. Against the Gnostics who would resolve Christ's humanness into an unreality he argues that for his work to be for us, 'the sacrament of man's redemption,'[2] Christ must needs have been born as man 'capable of death.'[3] Only in the form of a man could he do the one thing required for man's salvation, so that the corruption of our nature be cleansed by his blood, and the grace lost by our offending God be restored by his death. Thus in Christ's death, 'lies the whole weight and fruit of the Christian name.'[4]

Helmut Thielicke has a section in his systematic theology entitled: 'The Depth of Humanity: the Cross' in which he explores the significance of Christ's perfect human existence for the Christian gospel. He declared that Christ exposed himself to mutability because of his love: 'What makes him unique - the unreservedness of his love - also makes him like all of us.'[5] In love, all that human flesh could endure he endured. Thielicke dwells on the physical pain and torture of Golgotha to render void any docetic view of Christ's person. He consequently asserts that Christ is a loving subject because he gives himself wholly and unreservedly, because he holds nothing back and leaves no way out, whether in the form of twelve legions of angels (Matthew 26:53), or of a supernatural docetic margin which sees to it that he escapes the final solidarity of suffering, that this touches only the human livery, and not the body itself (Job 2:4f.).[6]

It is, then, 'in the body of his flesh by his death' (Col. 1:22) that Jesus achieved man's reconciliation to God. As true man he came to live as God's man among us and died as God's man for us. By piling up his terms, 'Christ's physical body through death' (NIV) Paul is not indulging in a needless exuberance of language. For the phrase is, in truth,

> just the right expression needed to understand the physical cost of the Church's redemption, which is achieved, not with a wave of the hand, or some automatic process, but by the coming of God in the person of his Son to the world, his clothing himself in our humanity and, then, suffering the bitterness and shame of a death on the cross - because of his affinity with humanity in its need.[7]

George Smeaton considers the statement 'in the body' as affirming Christ's true corporeity, and the phrase 'of his flesh' as declaring that, 'He carried about on earth a sin-bearing humanity, and therefore a weak, abased and suffering humanity'. When all the elements of the passage are put together he concludes, 'the apostle's testimony here amounts to this, that the atonement was consummated historically and once for all in the person of the incarnate, abased and dying Surety; and it takes in His life, wound up by His death (verses 20, 22).'[8]

It may be that Paul had in mind the docetism of the heretical teachers who asserted that our Lord's body was only a phantom or appearance. They declared the body of Jesus unreal, not authentic. The apostle's words may have been intended to counteract such a false notion and to insist that it was a truly human nature that the Son of God assumed at the incarnation, as it was the same genuine human body that underwent the death of the cross. The words remain, however, as a correction of those who like John McLeod Campbell locate the significance of Christ's atonement solely in the spiritual and moral condition of the one who endured the suffering of the cross. But since God's verdict on man the sinner in his judgement on sin relates to the individual in the totality of his existence, it is required that Christ should meet in full the necessities of man's full reconciliation. While our Lord's sufferings were, indeed, those of the spirit that was his, they were no less those of the body that was his.

> He bowed his head in solemn submission to God's sentence upon it (sin), and tasted death for every man. It is in this sense and not only

in a 'merely' or 'purely' spiritual one, that he bore our sins. The New Testament uniformly takes this for granted. But he bore them in his heart supremely in the act and instance of bearing them in his body on the tree, and it is not in distinguishing these two truths, and still less by denying either, but insisting upon their indissoluble interpenetration that we touch the nerve of Christ's reconciling power.[9]

Incarnate Deity

Yet while in the cross Christ was present as man fully, as man's representative and substitute, he was not there as man only. For he was there as the Son of God made flesh (John 1:14), born of woman (Gal. 4:4). He was there as 'this man' (Heb. 3:1; 7:24; 10:12) in whom dwells all the fullness of the deity bodily (Col. 2:9). This truth of Christ as man truly, yet not man only, brings another dimension to the Calvary event than that of the death of a good human. For not only does Jesus as man suffer there at the hands of wicked men, but in some mysterious way the Godhood that was his suffered in him on account of man's sin. In this regard, it is to be noted that it is in the wider context of the reconciling work of Christ in the body of his flesh through death that Paul affirms that in him dwells the whole fullness of the deity *bodily* (Col. 2:9). The heretics had dethroned Christ to a place of one among their many mediators. The apostle enthrones him as alone the One in whom 'God gives a full and complete expression of himself' (Phillips). Therefore, Paul wants it understood that what was present in Christ was not a mere characteristic of the divine nature. Christ was not just a godlike man. By employing the genitive form *Theotestos* - of deity - he was affirming that it was the whole essence and nature of God in their unbounded power and fullness which resides in him. It means nothing less than 'the quality of divine being' (Lohse) that had 'fixed abode' in Jesus Christ, the Lord.

The term *pleroma* - fullness - appears to have been one of the heretics' special words. It was used by them as a solution to the problem of the relation between God and the world,

a system of intermediate links between the two made up of the *pleroma*. Paul accepts this premise and the need for mediation, but quickly demolishes any spurious claims to a hierarchy of intermediaries (the aeons) by roundly asserting that all the *pleroma* is in Christ; and moreover this fullness is of the one divine essence so that Christ's office as a go-between is perfect since he is true God, true man.'[5]

The fullness of the deity is said to be in Christ bodily. In a human body, 'incarnately' (Abbott), 'corporeally' (Lightfoot), is the totality of the divine nature forever seen and forever secured in him. Here 'really, not symbolically', 'actually, not apparently' is God known as the God of salvation and man reconciled in the reconciliation achieved in 'Christ's physical body by his flesh'. The *pleroma* dwells in him *bodily*; not in a body opposed to the spirit, but in a body opposed to the shadow. Yet it was not merely 'into' a body that he came, but he actually and literally became flesh and blood by a true incarnation: 'assuming the nature of a slave. Bearing the human likeness, revealed in human shape' (Phil. 2:7, 8 NEB).

It would seem that Paul wishes to stress the reality of the union of the Son of God with human flesh in view of the heretics' repudiation of the body as of any worth. Paul saw the reconciliation effected by Christ as touching the whole life. Hence his stress on the bodily residence of the total fullness of the deity in him. So is the reconciliation enacted in the physical body of him in whom dwells the fullness of deity in bodily form at once the renewal of man's spirit to eternal life and the redemption of his body to resurrection certainty. Thus is the saving work of God through the Calvary event at one with the atoning work of Christ; and, vice versa, the reconciling work of the Father with the saving work of the Son.

There are two other passages in the New Testament which relate the atoning act to the sin-bearing body of Christ. The Epistle to the Hebrews speaks of Christ's 'offering of [his] body once for all' (Heb. 10:10) to 'bear the sins of many' (Heb. 9:28), and Peter declares that, 'He [Christ] himself bore our sins in his body on the tree' (1 Pet. 2:24). Each writer uses the same Greek word regarding Christ's 'bearing' of man's sin; and the same significance is to be attached to its use in both passages. The word enshrines the thought of Isaiah 53:12, 'yet he bore the sin of many', and carries the idea of the sin-bearing action of the Lord's Servant, of Jesus Christ, the Son of God. The thought is that he took sin as a load upon himself to bear its full weight and consequences to the cross. Thus is Christ's atoning act to be conceived of as a sin-bearing act effected 'in his body' which he offered in sacrifice for the sins of the world.

The phrase 'in his body' of Hebrews 10:10 and 1 Peter 2:24 re-echoes the words of 1 Corinthians 11:24, ' "This is my body which is for you" ', which in turn recall our Lord's words, ' "This is my body, broken for you"' (Cor. 11:24 AV). Some theologians and commentators distinguish between the saving work of Christ's shed blood and the offering of his body, and suggest that it is by the blood of Christ we are reconciled to God and by his offering of his body we are made holy. The former concerns our acceptance and acquittal from sin; the latter our perfection and holiness by union with Christ and participation in his Spirit. This is, perhaps, to introduce too fine a distinction. True, the text of Hebrews 10:10 does declare that 'we have been sanctified through the offering of the body of Jesus Christ once for all'. But it would seem that for the writer of Hebrews sanctification 'through the offering of the body of Christ', is one and the same with the Pauline declaration of our being 'justified by his blood'.

The sanctification of which the writer speaks is related to Christ's work accomplished in the Calvary event. We have been sanctified when 'Christ had offered for all time a single sacrifice for sins' (Heb. 10:12; cf. v. 14). So were we sanctified and justified in the name of our Lord Jesus Christ and in the Spirit of our God (1 Cor. 6:11). Thus does God become 'the source of your life in Christ Jesus, whom God made our wisdom, our righteousness and sanctification and redemption' (1 Cor. 1:30). Our sanctification in the offering of the body of Christ is what our redemption is by the blood of his cross; while the reconciliation achieved 'in his body of flesh by his death' of Colossians 1:22 is at one with the shedding of 'his own blood, thus securing an eternal redemption,' of Hebrews 9:12. Both assure us that in the atoning act of Christ we have our reconciliation and redemption as the ground for the forgiveness of our sins (cf. Col. 1:14; Heb. 10:17-18) and our access to God (Rom. 5:2; Eph. 2:18; Heb. 4:16; cf. 9:24). Thus do the declarations of Paul, 'he has now reconciled in his body of flesh by his death' (Col. 1:22); of Peter, 'He himself bore our sins in his body on the tree' (1 Pet. 2:24); of the Epistle to the Hebrews, 'We have been sanctified through the offering of the body of Jesus Christ once for all' (Heb. 10:10), feature a doctrine of the atonement, objective and once for all in the work of Christ, in which sin has been dealt with in the death of Christ, our reconciliation to God achieved and that holiness without which no man can see God made available to faith.

Only in a body 'prepared' for him could the Son of God offer himself as the one perfect sacrifice to God for the salvation of man. Only in a body could he be for us our representative and substitute. Only in a body could he shed his blood for the remission of sin. Only in a body could his vicarious sin-bearing action in the Calvary event be a reality of history.

Thus did the Son of God, by the Father's appointment, in full obedience come among mankind as man by connecting himself with sinful humanity; and in this associating himself with man's existence and condition he incorporated fallen humanity with himself in the body of his flesh. He made our sins his own by taking them on himself as if they were all his own so that he met in himself, in the body of his flesh through death, God's holy judgement on sin and the burden of its guilt. The incarnate Son, in his sinless humanity, gave himself in the sacrifice of the cross to expiate sin. He accepted and fulfilled every requirement on God's part and every condition of man's for our reconciliation to God and the forgiveness of our sins. 'For God has done what the law, weakened by the flesh, could not do: sending his own Son in the likeness of sinful flesh and for sin, he condemned sin in the flesh' (Rom. 8:3).

Notes

1. cf. McDonald, (1966) *I and He*, London, Epworth Press, McDonald (1986) 'Biblical Teaching on Personality' in Jonnnes, Stanton L. (ed.) *Psychology and the Christian Faith*, Grand Rapids, Baker.
2. Tertullian, *Adv. Marcionem*, ii, 27.
3. Tertullian, *De Carne Christi*, 5.
4. *Adv. Marcionem*, iii, 3.
5. Thielicke, Helmut, *The Evangelical Faith*, ed. and tr. (1974-82) Barber, C.C. and Bromiley, G.W., Grand Rapids, Eerdmans: (1978) Edinburgh, T. & T. Clark, ii, 383.
6. *ibid.*
7. Martin, R.P., (1972) *Colossians, The Church's Lord and the Christian's Liberty*, Grand Rapids, Zondervan: Exeter, Paternoster Press.
8. Smeaton, George, (1957) *The Apostle's Doctrine of the Atonement*, Grand Rapids, Zondervan, 302.
9. Denney, J., (1911) *The Christian Doctrine of Reconciliation*, London, Hodder & Stoughton, 274.
10. Martin, *op. cit.*

Chapter VII
A LAMB SLAIN

The title 'The Lamb of God' (John 1:29), put at the beginning of the fourth Gospel, is meant to convey the writer's own understanding of the significance of the person and work of Christ. At the time of John the Baptist's declaration the belief was widespread that the Messiah was about to come. Some even questioned the Baptist whether indeed he himself was not the expected one. But he emphatically denied it, ' "I am not the Christ" ' - not the Messiah - he insisted (John 1:20). The next day, seeing Jesus coming towards. him he said in the presence of his disciples,' "Behold the Lamb of God, who takes away the sin of the world!" ' (John 1:29.) Thus at the outset of his ministry Jesus as Messiah was identified as the Lamb of God. It must, consequently, be the case that the declaration 'the Lamb of God' was intelligible to those who heard it. The idea of the Messiah as the Lamb of God was not strange in their ears. For, as Godet points out, the association of the Servant of the Lord of Isaiah with the lamb of chapter 53:7 was for long general among Jewish commentators.[1] It was only after Christians had appealed to the correctness of this identity that Jewish commentators, in their polemic against its fulfilment in the person and work of Christ, sought another explanation in an effort to nullify their proclamation.

Lamb of God
Twice in John's Gospel Christ is called 'the Lamb of God' (1:29,35) and on both occasions by John the Baptist. The word used, *amnos*, lamb, is found also in Acts 8:32 and 1 Peter 1:19 and in the LXX version of Isaiah 53:7. Many commentators, noting this last fact, see the 'lamb led to the slaughter' of Isaiah's prophecy as providing the immediate context for an interpretation of the Baptist's declaration. Thus A.F. Delitzsch states categorically, 'All the utterances in the New Testament regarding the Lamb of God are derived from this prophecy (Isa. 53:7) in which the dumb type of the Passover now finds a tongue.'[2] In this regard it is to be noted that Philip, in his encounter with the Ethiopian eunuch, immediately declared Isaiah 53:7 to be a prophecy of 'the good news of Jesus.' (Acts 8:29ff.)

In 1 Peter 1:19 Christ is likened to a lamb 'without blemish or spot' (cf. Lev. 14:10; 23:12, see v. 18; Num. 6:14, cf. 28:19; 29:2,8,20,29,32,36;

Ezek. 46:13). It is the precious blood of Christ, the Lamb of God, that is the ransom price for man's redemption from the futile ways and perishable things which dominate human life (1 Pet. 1:18). The allusion by Peter to the lamb 'without blemish or spot' suggests that while it is acceptable to take Isaiah 53:7 as holding the key to its meaning, the interpretation of the title the Lamb of God must not be restricted to that passage. There is a richer and fuller interpretation of the title which goes beyond this verse. Thus Westcott, in his careful exegesis of John 1:29, while accepting Isaiah 53:7 as the main Old Testament background of the designation, does not limit its significance thereto. Noting that the Baptist had already made reference to Isaiah, Westcott points out that such an allusion, 'might naturally lead to inquiries as to the general scope of the prophet', although there is 'no doubt that the image is derived from Isaiah Liii.'[3] He later adds that the idea of vicarious suffering conveyed by the prophet's language does not exhaust the meaning of the image. He refers to the lamb, the victim offered at the morning and evening sacrifice (Exod. 29:39ff.) And especially, in the light of the fact that at the time the Baptist spoke the Passover was not far off (John 2:12-13), he regards it as impossible to exclude the paschal lamb with which our Lord was later identified (cf. John 19:36). The deliverance from Egypt, a notable display of God's redeeming grace in which the sprinkling of blood had a conspicuous place, is an eloquent symbol of the saving work of the Messiah.

We have suggested elsewhere[4] that too much energy seems to be expended in seeking to link what the Baptist declared concerning Christ with a limited and specific Old Testament passage. The fact is, rather, that a lamb having relation to the sin, need and worship of the people had, throughout the progressive revelation of God's unfolding plan of salvation, a particular reference. If Exodus tells us of the necessity of the lamb, then Leviticus may be said to specify its purity for sacrifice; it must be a lamb without blemish. Isaiah focuses on the personality of the lamb as the Servant of the Lord. *He* it is who is brought as a lamb to the slaughter. It was left to the Baptist, the last of the prophets, to affirm his identity as the Lamb of God, the Messiah, the greater than he. John most surely must have regarded the Messiah as God's lamb in the light of Isaiah's prophecy and specifically as the one on whom the Lord was laying the sins of the world. But he saw him, too, as gathering in himself all the strands of ancient ritual and Jewish prophecy relating to the lamb in the religion of Israel. In this one grand announcement the long evolution of the ages found at last - at God's right time - its culmination in a living person.

Commentators generally, however, take a more restricted view, opting for one or other of two favoured Old Testament passages. They divide unevenly, the greater number declaring for the slaughter lamb of Isaiah 53, and the rest for the paschal lamb of Exodus 12. Those who prefer this latter as its background do so, for the more part, because they are not prepared to admit a sacrificial significance attaches to the Baptist's word. They argue that the rite of Exodus 12 has no expiatory overtones. Exodus 12, is consequently, for them the certain background of the title the Lamb of God. Other commentators reject the reference precisely on the same grounds. However, it is not true that a sacrificial allusion is entirely absent from Exodus 12 in view of the words of verse 12: 'The blood shall be a sign for you . . . and when I see the blood, I will pass over you'. Perhaps, then, it is better to see the two figures of Isaiah 53:7 and of Exodus 12 as uniting in the Baptist's declaration of Christ as 'the Lamb of God'. They are not contradictory; they are complementary. At any rate, in both instances, whether that of Christ as the Lamb of God or of Christ as likened to a lamb without blemish or spot, there is affirmed something to be done for man's salvation. It is this 'something done' by the one to whom the symbol 'lamb' is applied that is our present concern. Following through the suggestion advanced by the majority of scholars that in John the Baptist's words the thought uppermost is of the lamb of Isaiah 53:7 we are justified in taking the title, the Lamb of God, as specifying Christ as the lamb of the atoning death. In 1 Peter 1, the allusion to the 'sprinkling with his blood' in v. 2, and Christ likened to a lamb, would seem to have a backward glance to Exodus 12. In that case we can truly speak of Christ as the lamb of the sacrificial blood.

For the first of these, the lamb of the atoning death, the prophetic vision of Isaiah has significance. The messianic figure in Isaiah is identified as the Servant of the Lord, yet as one closely associated with God in his acts of salvation. As the Servant of the Lord by God's appointment he is further identified with the lamb led to the slaughter of Isaiah 53:7. This fate was not just the result of man's plotting; it was of God's planning. For in being wounded for our transgression and bruised for our iniquities, he was stricken, smitten of God and afflicted. It was of the Lord to lay upon him the transgressions and iniquities of us all. Yet he was as the lamb who gave 'himself an offering for sin' (v. 10); and by his wounds and in his dying he 'bore the sin of many'. This is the one whom John the Baptist introduces as the Lamb of God. He had come forth from God to do the Father's will. And in fulfilment of that will he was led to Calvary: and there on the cross on the green hill he bore our sins in his body to the tree (1 Pet. 2:24).

The use of the genitive of possession - the Lamb of God - specifically relates, the Christ, the Messiah, to God. As the Servant of the Lord of Isaiah's prophecy he fulfils a sin-bearing act. The Lamb of God

> is more than a victim God provides, as he provided a ram. in the place of Isaac (Gen. 22:8) . . . (for) in the coming of Christ God

himself is active; he not only accepts an offering made by man but he provides (for indeed he himself is) the offering, and he himself made it.'[5]

More strictly it should be stated, 'Christ is the lamb of God. that is, the lamb God himself furnishes for sacrifice'.[6] Christ, who is of God and whose relation to God was that of equality with God before the world was called into existence, and who was the very divine word of its creation (John 1:2), took flesh and entered human history as the Lamb of God to offer himself to God for the sin of the world. He is at once the atoning victim presented to God and the sacrificial victim provided by God. 'The assertion that a murdered Jesus is the Lamb of God who takes away the sin of the world is too great not to be true, and the verification of it has been too wonderful to let us suppose it false.'[7] 'A lamb that takes away sin is a sacrificial lamb, and it is not serious when one affects to find anything else here than what is suggested by the *hilasmos* of the epistle or the *hilasterion* of Paul.'[8] Westcott affirms that, 'the title applied to Christ (the Lamb of God) under the circumstances of its utterance, conveys the ideas of vicarious sufferings, of patient submission, of sacrifice, of redemption.'[9] So is the Christ, the lamb of God's providing, the Saviour, the lamb of sin's atonement. Such was the sole reason for the Lamb's appearance on the stage of human history. He came to deal with the awful reality of human sin and the consequences of that fateful fall which brought into human existence all our woes.

The singular *sin* in the EVV and best manuscripts, rather than 'sins' as in the Episcopal Prayer Book, is to be stressed. For Christ's work has a nullifying effect on sin as the one conditioning principle of sins: on its root, and not simply on its fruit. In his vicarious action as the Lamb of God he uprooted the tree, he did not just cut off its branches. He appeared to put away sin, once for all, by the sacrifice of himself. It was with the sin of the world that the Lamb's sacrifice is concerned. The world made by him (John 1:10) had become marred by human sin. To meet the atoning necessities for the creation of a new world in which dwells righteousness, the Lamb of God has taken away sin by bearing on himself the total load of it. In Christ. as the lamb of God's own providing, God was reconciling the world unto himself. More specifically, however, the Baptist's words have reference to the world as summed up in sinful humanity and so separated from God (cf. John 8:12; 9:5; 1 John 4:9) and hostile to him (John 14:17; 15:18).

In this one grand announcement that the Lamb of God takes away the sin of the world, the Baptist sets forth the excellence of the sacrifice (the Lamb of God), its efficacy (takes away sin), and its extent (the world). The only fitting response is to cry with the hosts of heaven, ' "Worthy is the lamb who was slain" ' (Rev. 5:12).

Uppermost in the mind of Peter, when he declares that our redemption is 'with the precious blood of Christ, like that of a lamb without blemish or spot' (1 Pet. 1:19) would seem to be the lamb of the Passover ritual of Exodus 12. As such, Christ is the lamb of the sacrificial blood. The Passover was a yearly feast on the part of Israel to celebrate their deliverance from Egypt and their safety from its plagues within their blood-sprinkled sanctuaries. It is for such 'sprinkling with the blood of Christ' that believers are chosen and destined to sanctification by the Spirit and obedience to Christ (1 Pet. 1:2). The precious blood of Christ, like a lamb without blemish or spot, is the ransom price of our deliverance and safety. In the efficacy of the blood of Christ there is both peace with God and the energy of live in that peace. A devout commentator of an earlier date makes the observation on 1 Peter 1:18-19:

> As it is misery to be liable to the sentence of death, so it is slavery to be subject to the dominion of sin; and he that is delivered from the one is likewise set free from the other. There is one redemption for both. He that is redeemed from destruction by the blood of Christ, is likewise redeemed from that sin and unholy conversation (way of life) which leads to it. Our redemption was appointed for this purpose, not to free the captives from sentence of death and leave them still in prison, but to proclaim liberty to the captives, and the opening of the prison to them that are bound. (Isaiah 61:1).[10]

The Lamb upon the Throne

In the Book of Revelation the redeeming action of Christ is strongly stated in the use of the title 'the Lamb'. The term occurs 28 times and is a diminutive form peculiar to the Apocalypse, although it is found in the fourth Gospel but not in reference to Christ (John 21:15). The use of a different term that has not immediate overtones of the Levitical sacrificial system seems to allow the writer to give a wider significance to it. In Revelation we seem to be moving in a different dimension of ideas; into a region of symbolism and prophecy where the imagination needs wings of flight and where exact logical thought can only plod along on foot. Yet there is a dominant thought undergirding and overarching the whole apocalyptic vision of the seer of Patmos; it is the concept of the sovereign redeemership of the exalted Lamb present in history. As such, he is related to history as the royal Lamb of sovereignty and the sacrificial Lamb of redemption. In the fifth chapter this combination of sovereignty and sacrifice is tellingly presented in John's sudden change of vision between a 'lion' and a 'lamb'. In the hand of him who sat upon the throne was a sealed scroll and John heard the angel call for someone, whether in heaven, on earth, or under the earth, worthy to loose its seals to do so. Then there appeared, in the midst of the four-and-twenty elders and the four living creatures, the Lion of the tribe of Judah, in symbolism of overwhelming power and sovereign majesty, who broke the seals and opened the book. But as John looked again it was now not a lion but 'a lamb standing as though it had been slain'. Thus is the symbol of the lion in its strength merged into that of the sacrificial lamb. In the midst of the throne in heaven is the throne of God and of the Lamb (22:1,3). At the heart of God's sovereignty is the reality of sacrificial love.

It is specifically, however, under the figure of the suffering lamb that the redemptive action of Christ's work is presented in Revelation. John opens his Apocalypse with what is virtually a doxology. That was, indeed, the proper beginning for him who was so sure of the love of God and release from sin, that he can recall the means, 'by his [Christ's] blood' by which that love has been assured and peace with God secured. He is about to invoke grace and peace on the churches from God the Father through Jesus Christ 'the faithful witness, the first-born of the dead, and the ruler of kings on earth.' But immediately his mind turns back to the Calvary event in which God was revealed as grace in his love and as peace in sin's atonement. Such is the import of his words: 'To him who loves us and has freed us from our sins by his blood' (1:5). The verb *love* is in the present continuous tense, for God's love remains forever, unchanged and unchanging; but liberation from sin is in the past tense, for he 'has freed us from our sins'. The act of liberation from sin was accomplished 'by his blood'. That looks back to the cross; and indicates, too, the cost - 'his blood'. The idea of his blood as the ransom price for our liberation is suggested by the very form of the words. It is even more explicitly stated in the new song of the redeemed. The Lion of the tribe of Judah, as the Lamb in the midst of the throne 'was slain' and by his blood 'didst ransom men for God' (5:9).

That blood shed as the means of our liberation from sin had its origin, its ground, and its working in the love of God. Such divine love has its manifestation in a region other than words. It is a love seen in action in the sacrifice of God's own Son, the Lamb of God.

> It is not any undefined goodwill, it is the love revealed in his dear-bought emancipation of the sinful, which inspires the doxology 'to him that loveth us'. Redemption it may be said springs from love, yet love is only a word of which we do not know the meaning till it is interpreted for us by redemption.'[11]

It is in the Calvary event that the love of God has its fittest announcement and its fullest manifestation. It is in the act of God in the Lamb that was slain that there lies the chief reason for the announcement 'God is love'. Only in the light of the cross can we speak meaningfully and truly of the love of God (cf. Rev. 1:5). In the sacrifice of Christ's death the wrath of God is overcome in the outflow of his love. The event of Calvary 'shows up both the seriousness of our position and the unspeakable wonder of Divine Love'. In the cross, 'the Son of God comes to us through the fiery barrier of the divine wrath; this is the compassion of God, which the gospel and it alone can make known to us.'[12] It is by the sacrifice of the Lamb that we have redemption (5:9), victory (12:11) and cleansing (7:14). It is because of the blood of the Lamb that our names are placed in the book of life (cf. 13:8; 21:27) - the names of those who have apprehended the redemption, victory and cleansing made effectual by the Lamb that was slain.

There is some dispute about the proper reference of the phrase 'before the foundation of the world' (13:8). The RSV refers it to the names not written in the Lamb's book of life, and so reads 'every one whose name has not been written before the foundation of the world in the book of life of the Lamb that was slain.' The NIV follows the AV to affirm the Lamb as the subject of the declaration: 'all whose names have not been written in the book of life belonging to the Lamb that was slain from the creation of the world.' James Denney contends that the former rendering is the correct one, and he states emphatically that,

> it is the names of the redeemed that stand from eternity in the Lamb's book of life not the death or sacrifice of the Lamb which is carried back from Calvary and invested with an eternal, as distinct from its historical, reality.[13]

Denney thinks that even the seer himself would have felt that the historical reality of the Calvary event would have been compromised by declaring the Lamb as slain before the foundation of the world. But Denney's argument against giving to the redeeming efficacy of the Lamb slain a timeless dimension does not seem sufficiently convincing. To do so does not compromise its historical actuality; both because of *who* the Lamb is, the Son of God, eternal with the Father, and *what* the Lamb accomplished in his sacrifice unto death by providing an 'eternal salvation' for mankind (Heb. 5:9). For John, the cross has a reach beyond the limited time and place of Calvary. After his resurrection Christ bore still the marks of his passion (John 20:24f.), and among the redeemed in glory the Lamb is present in the midst of the throne as it has been slain. From the crucifixion he carried the marks of the cost of man's salvation enacted in the historic present; but that cost borne by the Son of God's love which found expression in the historic event of Calvary was first a cross in the eternal heart of God. Thus for John, what was a fact of half a day was the truth of every day and the reality of the eternal day. For the cross is an act in time of timeless fact. John was sure that the Christ who wrought for man's sin a sacrifice of atonement was intimately related to God - the Lamb of God, the Lamb in the midst of the throne. He was of such a nature with God that what he did has the impress. the marks, the character and the value of God. For what he did at the place called Calvary has in it not only the finality of a historic but also the timelessness of a divine act. From the perspective of Christ's life in the flesh Calvary is a historical fact, while from the perspective of eternity it is a timeless act. So did Christ, the Lamb of God, accomplish in his death a full and perfect atonement for the sins of the world within the sphere of history, whilst at the same time securing for us eternal salvation.

Notes

1. Godet, (1899) *Commentary on St. John's Gospel*, (ET) Edinburgh, T. & T. Clark, i, 421.
2. Delitzsch, A. F., (1890)*Commentary on Isaiah*, (ET) Edinburgh, T. & T. Clark, ii, 297.
3. Westcott, B. F., (1900) *Gospel of St John*, London, John Murray.
4. McDonald, 'The Atonement of the Death of Christ', 73, cf. McDonald, 'The Lamb of God', in Elwell, Walter A. (ed.) *The Evangelical Dictionary of Theology*, Grand Rapids. Baker.
5. Temple, W., (1914) *Readings in St John's Gospel*; London, MacMillan, i, 24.
6. Westcott, *op. cit.*, 20.
7. Denney, James, (1911) *The Christian Doctrine of Reconciliation*, London, Hodder & Stoughton, 130.
8. *ibid.*, 175, 176.
9. *ibid.*, Westcott.
10. Leighton. Robert, *A Practical Commentary on the First Epistle of St Peter*, London, 160-161.
11. Denney, (1911) *The Death of Christ*, (rev. edn), London, Hodder & Stoughton, 176.
12. Brunner, Emil, (1934) *The Mediator*, tr. Wyon, O., London, Lutterworth, 487.
13. Denney, *op. cit.*, 180.

Chapter VIII
AS A PASSOVER CELEBRATED

It was suggested earlier that there is an allusion to the Passover lamb in Peter's reference to the sprinkling of the blood of Christ (1 Pet. 1:2; cf. Exod. 12:7,13), and the 'lamb without blemish or spot' (1 Pet. 1:19; cf. Exod. 12:5). Some New Testament scholars, however, profess to find numerous obscure and hidden allusions to the Passover feast in 1 Peter. They regard the epistle as a paschal liturgy connected with preparation for Easter baptismal ceremonies which were widely practised in the early church.[1] This view has not, however, won wide acceptance; and the allusions besides are too indefinite to permit dogmatism. But even if this were granted the allusions are not specific enough to shed much light on the apostle's statements of the need and efficacy of the precious blood of Christ, the paschal lamb, for our ransom from the futile ways of fallen human existence. If, then, what we have, at most, in Peter's epistle are interpretative allusions to the Passover, there is in Paul's First Epistle to the Corinthians a definite expression of the work of Christ in Passover terms. The apostle's word is, 'Cleanse out the old leaven that you may be a new lump, as you really are unleavened. For Christ, our paschal lamb' ('our passover' AV; 'our passover lamb' NIV) 'has been sacrificed' (1 Cor. 5:7).

Some scholars believe that Paul wrote 1 Corinthians at the time of Passover, when the offering of the paschal lamb and the sprinkling on the door lintels was much in the minds of the Jewish worshipping community. It is supposed, then, that the apostle,

Perhaps for the very first time was quick to see an illustration of Christ and his redeeming work in the sacrifice of the lamb and, in the complete removal of leaven which preceded the feast (Ex. 12:18), an illustration of the moral purification which Christianity called for.[2]

The annual celebration of the Passover festival rested, certainly, on the offering of the paschal lamb; and it is beyond doubt that the sacrifice was conceived, in common with others, (cf. Exod. 24:3-8), as having propitiatory power and atoning efficacy. But, perhaps, too much emphasis should not be placed on the suddenness of Paul's apprehension of Christ's sacrifice as that of a paschal lamb at this period of his contemplation of the gospel of the cross. He would have know already that the death of Christ took place at the Passover season, and he was probably aware of John's reference to the paschal lamb ('you shall not break a bone of it,' Exod. 12:46) as fulfilled in the crucifixion of Christ (John 19:36). And he knew, too, that Christ himself had made a connection between the Passover sacrifice of the lamb and the memorial feast of the Communion Supper.

Two Feasts

Two alternative terms are used in the New Testament to cover the ritual season of the Passover. One, the *pascha*, passed into common currency and is that by which the Passover feast is generally known. The other term *azumos*, which translated the Hebrew word for the Feast of the Unleavened Bread, is associated with it in the account of the first Passover (Exod. 12:17,18,20, cf. 3:7). In the New Testament both *pascha* and *azumos* are used to refer to the common festive season. Thus in the synoptic Gospels the designation 'Passover' occurs 16 times, and 'Unleavened Bread' five times. The fourth Gospel keeps exclusively to *Pascha* which is used on 10 occasions. In Mark 14:1 both terms are brought together: 'it was now two days before the Passover and the feast of Unleavened Bread.'

It is this conjunction of the two events of Passover and Unleavened Bread that Paul has in mind in the passage of 1 Corinthians 5:7-8. He has been dealing with the illegitimate boasting of the Corinthians, reminding them that such boasting was 'not good'. This foolish boasting would, if unchecked, spread to the destroying of their whole community life, as a little leaven ferments the whole lump of dough. The mention of leaven suggests to the apostle elements connected with the *pascha* feast which he uses typologically. He bids the Corinthian believers to 'purge out thoroughly' (*ekkatharate*) the old leaven, as the people of Israel were 'to put away leaven' out of their houses on the first day of the feast (Exod. 12:15). He sees malice and wickedness as 'old leaven' (v. 8). His reference to the 'old' is not found in the passover narrative, but is introduced by the apostle here to emphasise, by contrast, the leavening energy of the gospel (cf. Rom 7:6, Eph. 4:22,24; 2 Cor. 5:17). All this 'newness', all this 'leavening' can and should be ours because 'Christ, our paschal lamb, has been sacrificed'. The words in the AV text 'for us' (*huper hemon*) - 'For even Christ our passover is sacrificed *for us* (1 Cor. 5:7) are not in the best manuscripts. But enshrined in the word 'our' is the truth that Christ as the Passover lamb was slain on behalf of, and instead of, us.

The word for paschal lamb in the text is emphasised (cf. Mark 14:12; Luke 22:7). It is 'even Christ', Christ himself who is our Passover lamb; the one sacrificed as paschal lamb. Not, perhaps, so much in the term 'sacrificed' itself, as in the declaration of Christ as himself the paschal lamb is the atoning symbolism of the Passover rite clearly indicated. It was the 'lamb' and the 'blood' that truly constituted the Passover a real and acceptable sacrifice (cf. Exod. 12:27; 23:18; 2 Chron. 30:16).

The Hebrew noun *pascha*, derives from the verb *pasah* with the primary meaning 'to pass over' and so 'to spare', in the sense of deliverance from impending doom. Both in the Hebrew and the EVV there is a sort of word-play between the two expressions. 'It is the Lord's passover' (Exod. 12:11); 'and when I see the blood I will pass over you' (Exod. 12:13). And again, in Exodus 12:27, 'it is the sacrifice of the Lord's passover, for he passed over the houses of the people of Israel'. The Passover - the passing over - was effected in the 'blood'; and under the 'blood' of 'the sacrifice' the people had deliverance and safety.

Some writers on the religious climate of New Testament times suggest that almost certainly Jesus, in his capacity as a religious teacher (he was called Rabbi), would have been in attendance at the first Passover of his public ministry (cf. John 2:13), and there be called upon to take part in the *pascha* sacrifice. And again, in his last days, as he kept the Passover with his disciples he could well have offered the sacrifice it required. Thus a Hebrew Christian writer of deep spiritual insight points out that the first, the last, the only sacrifice which Jesus offered was that in which, symbolically, he offered himself. 'And,' he adds,

in truth, as we think of it, we can understand not only why the Lord could not have offered any other Sacrifice, but that it was most fitting he should have offered this one Pascha, partaking of its commemorative Supper, and connected his own New Institution with this to which the Supper pointed. This joining of the Old and the New, the one symbolic Sacrifice which he offered with the One Real Sacrifice, seems to cast light on the words with which he followed the expression of His longing to eat of the one Pascha with them: "I say unto you, I will not eat any more thereof, until it is fulfilled in the Kingdom of God." [3]

One sacrifice did Christ offer, that of the *pascha* lamb; which he as the Lamb of God himself truly was and whose sprinkled blood would be a shield of deliverance for all who came under its efficacy.

It is to be noted that the *pascha*, while truly a sacrifice, was distinctive. It was instituted before the law and the ratification of the covenant with blood. The *pascha*, in a sense was the cause and foundation of all the Levitical sacrifices and of the covenant itself. 'Just as the Priesthood of Christ was real, yet not after the order of Aaron, so was the Sacrifice of Christ real, yet not after the order of Levitical Sacrifices, but after that of the Passover.' [4]

This interpretation of Christ's death in terms of *pascha* sacrifice gives to it its fundamental place in the redemption of man. It is within the sanctuary of Christ's sprinkled blood that there is safety from the enemy of souls. For in that security all Israel - the new Israel of God - are saved. For ' "The Deliverer will come from Zion, he will banish ungodliness from Jacob; and this will be my covenant with them, when I take away their sins" ' (Rom. 11:26-7 quoting Isa. 59:20). It is in Christ, the slain Lamb of God's Passover, who was dead, but is now alive again, that there is deliverance from the wrath to come (1 Thess. 1:10).

Notes

1. Cross, F.L., (1954) *First Peter*, London, Mowbray.
2. Clements, J.C., (1915) 'Passover', in Hastings, J. (ed.) *Dictionary of the Apostolic Church*, ii, 134.
3. Edersheim, Alfred, (1897) *The Life and Times of Jesus the Messiah*, London, Longmans, ii, 491.
4. *ibid.*, 492.

Chapter IX
AS A COVENANT MADE

The main word for 'covenant' in the Hebrew Old Testament is *berith*. It occurs just over 300 times (excluding references to the 'tables', the 'ark', and the 'book' of the covenant). From its first use in Genesis 6:18 to its last in Malachi 3:1 it is translated *diatheke* in the Greek of the Septuagint. It is used on some occasions for an agreement between man and man (cf. Gen. 31:44) and a king and his people (e.g. 2 Kings 11:17; see 2 Chron. 23:16). In these instances the Old Testament term carries the idea of a mutual undertaking between two parties; but this connotation seems to be restricted to human relationships. By far the larger number of its occurrences relate to a covenant between God and selected representative individuals such as Noah (Gen. 6:18; cf. 9:9,10,11,13,15,16 etc.) Abraham (Gen. 15:18) and Moses (Exod. 34:10).

In reference to the covenant of God with mankind and Israel it has an explicit monopleuric (i.e. one-sided) connotation. Here the thought is that of the setting up of a relationship by the free choice and act of one party to make a covenant. When thus used of God's covenant-relationship with his people this monopleuric factor is absolute. The formula with which such a covenant is initiated and enacted is usually introduced with God's own declaration, ' "I will establish my covenant" ' (e.g. Gen. 6:18, 9:9, 11), or. ' "I will make my covenant" ' (e.g. Gen. 17:2). Uppermost, then, in the concept is that of a divine order transacted solely by God's free decision without any human cooperation. Akin to the word *berith* is *hesed*, which has inherent in it the thought of 'covenant love'; and which modern versions usually translate as 'steadfast love' where the KJV has 'mercy' (cf. Gen. 24:17: 32:10; Exod. 15:13; 20:6 etc. RSV). In several passages *berith* and *hesed*,˙ 'covenant' and 'steadfast love', occur together (e.g. Deut. 7:9,12; Neh. 1:5). It is on the basis of the steadfast love expressed in God's covenant with his people that Nehemiah prays for their restoration. God had allowed them to be delivered into the hand of their enemies because of their transgression and unfaithfulness. But Nehemiah can affirm in his pleadings to God on their behalf:

> Nevertheless in thy great mercies thou didst not make an end of them or forsake them; for thou art a gracious and merciful God. Now therefore, our God, the great and mighty and terrible God who

keepest covenant and steadfast love, let not all the hardship seem little to thee that has come upon us (Neh. 9:32).

It is not necessary, however, for our present purpose to go into a detailed exposition of the several covenants and their place in Old Testament religion except in so far as they relate to the interpretation of Christ's work. The large number of instances of covenant in the Old Testament has led writers such as Eichrodt to take the covenant concept as the guiding principle of its theology. The same fact has inspired the attempt of several systematic theologians to subsume their dogmatics within a covenantal framework. This theological methodology, which would identify a number of succeeding historical covenant's stemming from a pre-existing one between God the Father and the Son - which they would identify with the 'eternal covenant' of Hebrews 13:20 - was first proposed by the Swiss reformers Zwingli and Bullinger, and given classical statement by Olevetanus in his 'Concerning the Nature of Covenant Between God and the Elect' (1588) and Cocecius in his 'Doctrine of the Covenant and Testament of God' (1648). This approach was taken up in the Westminster Confession of 1646 where the doctrine of Christ's work is structured according to God's 'covenanted' acts (cf. chs. x-xvii). The claim that Calvin's *Institutes of the Christian Religion* is patterned after the same fashion can hardly be sustained. In fact in the detailed index of the two-volumed translation by Henry Beveridge the term 'covenant' does not once appear. The covenant principle would seem too narrow a concept into which to fit the entire significance of the Calvary event.

Nevertheless, Christ's work must be related to the covenant concept, if for no other reason than that Christ himself at the institution of the Last Supper so connected it. In the Greek of the New Testament the LXX word for covenant, *diatheke*, occurs 33 times. In its soteriological contexts the covenant is conceived of as God's unilateral enactment. This fact has led some New Testament scholars to suggest the idea of 'will' as better conveying the significance of the term. There are, indeed, passages both in Paul's epistles and the Epistle to the Hebrews where the translators pass from the one English term - will or covenant - to the other (e.g. Gal. 3:15-17; Heb. 9:16-18). The statement by the apostle Paul in Galatians 3:15. 'To give a human example, brethren: no one annuls even a man's will, or adds to it, once it has been ratified', is of special interest in this connection. The word translated 'will' in the RSV text is the same as that translated 'covenant' in the AV, 'contract' in Phillips. This serves to underscore the one-sidedness of the transaction involved. The terms of a 'will' are made unilaterally and when signed and sealed are binding. In his 'covenant', ratified by the death of Christ and sealed by his blood, God undertakes to fulfil its every pledge.

Of the 33 occurrences of the term *diatheke* in the New Testament, 14 have a specific reference to the person and work of Christ. Christ is the mediator of the new covenant (Heb. 9:15; cf. 8:6; 12:24) and its surety (Heb. 7:22). Like the earlier covenants, the 'new covenant' (Heb. 7:22) 'was not ratified without blood' (Heb. 9:18). It is thus to Christ we come as 'the mediator of a new covenant, and to the sprinkled blood that speaks more graciously than the blood of Abel' (Heb. 12:24).

New Covenant

The qualification 'new' in connection with the covenant instituted by the person and work of Christ in Hebrews 8:8 and 9:15 (cf. Matt. 26:28) turns attention to the messianic prophecies of the Old Testament and the 'new covenant' foreshadowed by Jeremiah. In Isaiah 42:6-7, the Servant of the Lord (cf. v.1) is given by God 'as a covenant to the people, a light to the nations, to open the eyes that are blind, to bring out the prisoners from the dungeon, from the prison those who sit in darkness' (cf. Isa. 49:8). The significance of the Servant of the Lord in relation to the covenant can be variously assessed depending on whether the stress is put upon the first phrase in the statement, 'a covenant', or the second, 'to the people'. If it is on the first, then it is the Servant in his person as Servant who is the instrument in enacting the covenant between God and his people; if on the second, 'to the people', then the Servant will be seen as the means of establishing the covenant which by God's action changes the people's condition. Clearly, the Servant of the Lord of Isaiah 49:8 is to be identified with the Servant of Isaiah 53 (cf. 52:13). Such is the one wounded for our transgressions and bruised for our iniquities. Like a lamb led to the slaughter it was the Lord's will 'to bruise him' and to 'put him to grief' (53:10).

In his synagogue sermon at Nazareth (Luke 4:17-21) Christ identified himself as the Servant of the Lord. In making that identification, there must have been in his mind the thought of himself as the inaugurator of the new covenant and of the substance of that covenant as enacted by his death as he gave himself an offering for sin. So, according to F.C. Fensham, Christ's sacrifice on the cross is the most important part of the formation of the new covenant. Paul correctly interpreted Christ's crucifixion as taking on him the curse of the law in order to redeem mankind (Gal. 3:13). With the new covenant the curse of the old Sinaitic covenant is removed by Christ.[1]

In Jeremiah 31:31-34, the prophet envisions the dawn of a more glorious future for the people of God. The whole passage reads:

Behold, the days are coming, says the Lord, when I will make a new covenant with the house of Israel and the house of Judah, not like the covenant which I made with their fathers when I took them by the hand to bring them out of the land of Egypt, my covenant which they broke, though I was their husband, says the Lord. But this is the covenant which I will make with the house of Israel after those days, says the Lord: I will put my law within them, and I will write it upon their hearts; and I will be their God, and they shall be my people. And no longer shall each man teach his neighbour and each his brother, saying, "Know the Lord," for they shall all know me, from the least of them to the greatest, says the Lord; for I will forgive their iniquity, and I will remember their sin no more.

Reflection on this passage will bring out three factors in connection with the 'new covenant' which have their realisation in the person and work of Christ. First, there is the absolute certainty of its fulfilment. The bringing in of the new covenant is declared to be God's own promised action: 'Says the Lord, I will make a new covenant'. The 'I' of the promise is the I AM of eternal truth and righteousness. He is the God of 'steadfast love'. The writer of the Epistle to the Hebrews, quoting the whole passage of Jeremiah 31:31-34, prefaces it with the observation, 'but as it is, Christ has obtained a ministry which is as much more excellent than the old as the covenant he mediates is better, since it is enacted on better promises. For if that first covenant had been faultless, there would have been no occasion for a second' (Heb. 8:6f.). Some centuries after Jeremiah had promised a new covenant, 'when the time had fully come, God sent forth his Son, born of woman' (Gal. 4:4). In him all the promises of God for the salvation of man have their 'Yea' and 'Amen' (cf. 2 Cor. 1:20). So Zachariah, at the birth of Jesus. was 'filled with the Holy Spirit' and prophesied that in the coming of the Redeemer God had remembered his 'holy covenant' to Abraham (Luke 1:67f.: cf. v. 72). Thus are believers 'heirs' (Gal. 3:29), and 'children' (Gal. 4:28) of the promised 'new covenant' enacted in the Calvary event.

Second, there is the radical emphasis on inwardness. The covenant which God had made with the fathers of Israel was for the most part concerned with external things, with outward acts of transgression and the breaching of the ceremonial law. The blessings accruing besides were for the most part more in the nature of temporal blessings and national prosperity. The new covenant, by contrast, has concern with the deep-down affairs of human life, with the centre of man's being where sin has its ultimate lodgement in his conscience and heart. In contrast, therefore, with the sacrifices of the old economy, 'how much more shall the blood of Christ, who through the eternal Spirit offered himself without blemish to God, purify your conscience from dead works to serve the living God' (Heb. 9:14). Being thus purged 'we have confidence to enter the sanctuary by the blood of Jesus' and we are able to 'draw near with a true heart in full assurance of faith' (Heb. 10:19-22).

Third, there is the final settlement of forgiveness. Within the community of the new covenant the least to the greatest would know the Lord with their iniquities forgiven and sins remembered no more (Jer. 31:34). No longer would their iniquities and sins come into view in the daily and yearly sacrifices of the ritual of the old covenant. In the new covenant forgiveness is absolute and full. For the sacrifice which procures it is once and for all (Heb. 7:27). Christ has appeared to put away sin *once for all* by the sacrifice of himself (Heb. 9:26). He was *once* offered to bear the sins of many (Heb. 9:28) 'For Christ also died for sins *once for all*, the righteous for the unrighteous that he might bring us to God' (1 Pet. 3:18). Fulfilling the promise that God would forgive iniquity and remember sins no more, Christ has brought to us 'redemption through his blood for the forgiveness of sins' (Eph. 1:7; cf. Matt. 20:28).

All these factors connected with the promised new covenant of Jeremiah 31:31-34 are taken up and enshrined in Christ's declaration at the institution of the eucharistic memorial feast of bread and wine. He refers to the cup with the words, ' "this is my blood of the covenant, which is poured out for many for the forgiveness of sins" ' (Matt. 26:28). The event symbolised in the poured-out wine was soon to be fulfilled at Calvary. It is, of course, well known that some New Testament commentators do not accept that Christ could have made the full statement which, synthetised from the synoptic Gospels, reads: 'This is my blood of the new covenant poured out for you for the forgiveness of sins'. Mark is the authority for 'this is the blood of the covenant' and Luke for 'new' and 'is poured out'. But all three synopticists allude to the covenant. Bultmann is foremost among those who deny that Christ could have used the words which convey either the sacrificial idea, 'my blood of the new covenant', or that of the redemptive act, ('the blood) poured out for many'.[2] In this regard Bultmann was merely repeating the sceptical views of the early school of German liberal writers of whom Baur, Wrede, and Holtzmann were the most outspoken regarding what Christ could and could not have said.

Their main reason is the contention that, while Paul shows familiarity with the idea of a new covenant, there is no trace of any such awareness in the teaching of Jesus. For our part, however, it seems incredible, almost blasphemy, to assert so arrogantly what Jesus could and could not say. He had himself affirmed, ' "The word which you hear is not mine, but the Father's who sent me" ' (John 14:24; cf. 12:49). The Father had sent the Son and in him was reconciling the world unto himself: the Son was sent to accomplish the Father's purpose of salvation. Jesus had already announced that he must needs go to Jerusalem to suffer and die (Matt. 20:17-19). Indeed, he had already indicated that his purpose in doing so was to give his life a ransom for many (Matt. 20:28; Mark 10:45). He had also, in parable spoken of the sacrificial nature of his suffering and death as a bridegroom taken violently from a marriage feast (Matt. 9:15; Mark 2:10; Luke 5:35; cf. John 3:29) and as the beloved Son, sent last to the vineyard to execute his father's design, only to be cast out and killed (Matt. 21:39; Mark 12:8; Luke 20:15). But, as the bridegroom taken away, he would institute a new marriage feast, 'the marriage supper of the Lamb' (Rev. 19:9; cf. v. 7); and, as the beloved Son cast out and killed, he would still secure by that very death a heritage for 'the people of the promise'. In the course of his post-resurrection journey with the two disciples on the Annaus road, Jesus expounded to them in Moses and all the prophets the things concerning himself, telling them that to redeem Israel, - the new Israel - he had to have been condemned and crucified (Luke 24:27).

In the light of these facts (and more could be added), it is unwarranted to suggest that Jesus could not have conceived of himself as the mediator of a new covenant enacted in his own blood for the forgiveness of sins. He had come into the world for this purpose; to save his people from their sins (Matt. 1:21). And that saving act was actualised by him and affirmed in his own broken body and in his own shed blood. Accordingly, he interpreted the communion elements in terms of the new covenant for the forgiveness of iniquity and the remembrance of sin no more. In the broken bread and wine poured out the reality of Christ's sufferings and death has proclamation and efficacy. It can, then, be said categorically that the thirty-first chapter of Jeremiah, with its sublime prophecy of the new covenant, was present in the mind of Jesus as he poured out the wine with the words spoken, ' "This is my blood of the covenant." ' With the event of Calvary immediately in view Christ drew attention to his broken body and shed blood as the means of establishing a new covenant; a new relationship of God to man, in which remission of sins was its fundamental reason and its crowning blessing. In Christ's communion words 'my blood of the covenant' what was being taught in the sacrificial ritual of the old economy was affirmed - that covenant blood is sacrificial blood and in the blood shed is atoning efficacy.

If, for the sake of argument, it were granted (as we are not readily prepared to grant) that Jesus did not speak of his death as a 'new covenant', there is statement enough left to compel us to see some deep significance in that death. If all that Christ said as he broke the bread and poured out the wine was, ' "This is my body" ' and ' "This is my blood" ' there is enough in these words to alert his disciples to some sacrificial purpose in his broken body and in the shedding of his blood. When reflected upon after the resurrection and when contemplated with quickened spiritual insight, there was sufficient in these words to enable them to conclude that for their salvation something of divine moment was being enacted. His body was broken, 'he bare our sins in his own body on the tree' (1 Pet. 2:24). His blood was shed 'in whom we have redemption through his blood, the forgiveness of sins' (Eph. 1:7 AV). Enough was here to make the disciples aware that their soul's well-being depended on the sufferings and death to be endured by Christ at Calvary.

And again, should it be granted that the words 'new' and 'for the forgiveness of sins' were added later as an interpretative explanation of what Jesus said, 'still, if they are no more than this they are also not less. They are an interpretative expansion of a mind in a position naturally to know and understand what Jesus meant.'[3] And because Matthew alone links the covenant blood to the forgiveness of sins, it is not on that account restricted. For in truth,

> the passage (Matt. 26:28) answers all the modern sentimentalism that finds in the teaching of Jesus only pious ethical remarks or eschatological dreamings. He had a definite conception of his death on the cross as the basis of forgiveness of sin. The purpose of his blood of the new covenant was to remove (forgive) sins.[4]

It is grandly fitting, consequently, that the church should invoke from time to time as a benediction on its parting worshippers the words of Hebrews 13:20-21. The words echo our Lord's own statement of John 10:11, ' "I am the good shepherd. The good shepherd lays down his life for the sheep" ', and those he uttered at the institution of the Last Supper. ' "This is my blood of the [new] covenant which is poured out for you" ' (Matt. 26:28). In the benediction the everlasting covenant is referred specifically to the blood shed in the death of our Lord Jesus Christ. Yet now, as the living Lord, he makes effectual the saving terms of that covenant in the present life and experience of the believing community, to work in its constituent members to equip them for the doing of everything that is good in the sight of God. And all this, both as regards the enactment and benediction of the everlasting covenant, is 'through Jesus Christ; to whom be glory for ever, Amen'.

Notes

1. Fensham, F.C., (1990) 'Covenant', in Douglas, J.D. (ed.) *Illustrated Bible Dictionary*, London, Inter-Varsity Press, i, 330.
2. Bultmann, Rudolph, *The Theology of the New Testament*, London SCM i, 146f.
3. Denney, James, (1911) *The Death of Christ*, (rev. edn), London. Hodder & Stoughton, 38.
4. Robertson, A.T., (1930-33) *Word Pictures in the New Testament*. New York, Smith, i, 209, 210.

Chapter X
A SACRIFICE RENDERED

In spite of James Stewart's warning against accepting the principle 'that sacrifice, in the Levitical sense of the word, was the apostle's [Paul's] regulative concept'[1] in his interpretation of the Calvary event, there can be no doubt at all about the supreme place that the idea of sacrifice had in his thinking. Stewart considers it to be 'precarious exegesis' to seek 'a clue to Paul's doctrine of the cross in the supposed analogy of ancient sacrifices, Levitical or other.'[2] He allows nevertheless that it would be 'patently untrue' that 'thoughts of sacrifice were absent from Paul's mind as he meditated on the death of Christ.'[3] Certainly, such a denial could not be successfully maintained. It is, of course, true that in two places only in his epistles does the apostle use the term 'sacrifice' in reference to Christ's work. These two references are, however, specific and sufficient to make it evident that the concept supplied him with a form to interpret Christ's death in reference to sin. It is, indeed, not too much to say that in all the apostle affirms about the actuality and efficacy of the cross, the concept of sacrifice is there; sometimes in the foreground and always in the background of his thought.

In his own definite statements Paul declares, 'Christ loved us and gave himself up for us, a fragrant offering and sacrifice to God' (Eph. 5:2). In this declaration, which focuses on Christ's self-giving, two ideas of sacrifice are associated: anything presented to God is viewed as an offering, whilst an offering is something slain. In the other instance, 1 Corinthians 5:7, the backward glance at the Old Testament ritual is patent: 'For Christ our Passover Lamb is sacrificed for us' (NIV). While, however, these two passages are direct, there are other statements in which the background thought is accepted by many theologians and commentators to be the Old Testament sacrificial system. Such Pauline affirmations as he 'gave himself for us' (Gal. 1:4) and he 'died for us' (Rom. 5:8), which have a definite substitutionary connotation, belong to the category of sacrifice. The apostle's references, besides, to the blood of Christ as the ground of the benefits conferred by his death (Rom. 3:25; 1 Cor. 10:16; Eph. 2:13) can only be interpreted as 'sacrificial blood' (cf. Rom. 5:9; Eph. 1:7; Col. 1:20).

A like contention can be made with regard to some of Peter's statements in his First Epistle. The idea of sacrifice is present in Peter's allusion to the sprinkling of the blood of Jesus (1 Pet. 1:2; cf. Exod. 24:6); and 'you are redeemed . . . with the precious blood of Christ, a lamb without blemish or spot' (1 Pet. 1:18,19 NIV). 1 Peter 2:21-25 echoes the words of Isaiah 53:7f. in which the sacrificial idea of vicarious suffering is undoubted. In the Johannine writings the sacrificial aspect of Christ's death is present, even if not as all-pervasive as elsewhere. In the title the 'Lamb of God', whether the background thought is that of the paschal lamb of Exodus 12, or the ideal Servant of the Lord brought as a lamb to the slaughter (Isaiah 53:7), a sacrificial significance belongs to the title itself, as it does to the result of his action, 'to take away the sins of the world'.

Sacrifice in Hebrews

Of all the New Testament writings, however, the Epistle to the Hebrews makes the idea of sacrifice the master-key of its understanding of Christ's work. He fulfils, in his dying, all the functions of sacrifice. Everywhere, in fact, in the epistle, Christ's work is cast in the language of sacrifice. In the light of the cross Hebrews vindicates the principle, 'without the shedding of blood there is no forgiveness' (9:22). The repeated sacrifices of the Old Testament economy had written deeply on the hearts of God's people the idea that it is the blood that makes atonement for the soul (Lev. 17:11). The blood of Christ denotes a sacrifice of nobler name than the former ages knew anything about. The writer of the Epistle underscores the greatness and glory of Christ's person: 'of the son he says, "Thy throne, O God" ' (1:8); 'a priest for ever' (5:6), before declaring that he it was who brought in his sacrifice his 'so great salvation' for mankind. Thus did Christ offer himself (Heb. 10:14), in an offering consummated in his sacrifice (10:10). His offering was a sacrifice acceptable to God for our sins (Heb. 10:12). In his offering he sacrificed himself; and his sacrifice was his offering: 'Christ ... offered for all time a single sacrifice for sins' (10:12; cf. vv. 10,14). Thus, the once for all character of Christ's sacrifice is particularly connected in the epistle with the putting away of sins. In 9:26 and 10:12 the exclusive nature of Christ's offering is set against the endless repetitions of the Aaronic ritual expressed in terms of sacrifice.

The offering of sacrifice requires the presence of a priesthood. Christ is, consequently, set forth as, at the same time, the great high priest: the sole officient who offered himself as the one perfect sacrifice to God for our salvation (5:9; cf. 2:3; 9:28), cleansing (10:2; cf. 1:3) and sanctification (10:10,14). Therefore, Brunner rightly says, 'The most important sacrifice is that which is intended to remove some obstacle which has come between God and man: the atoning or expiatory sacrifice.'[4] And Christ's sacrifice was, indeed, the 'most important' because of who he was that rendered it, and because of what he achieved by it. Noting, then, the variety of references to and the implication of other terminology relating to Christ's atoning work, Warfield can justly affirm 'not only is the doctrine of the sacrificial death of Christ embodied in Christianity as an essential element of the system, but in a very real sense it constitutes Christianity.'[5] For the fact is that most of the terms in the New Testament which focus on the redemptive action of the Calvary event are associated with the altar and have a sacrificial connotation. Whatever a sacrifice is, such is the work of Christ. Not to recognise the sacrificial nature of Christ's work is not only to set aside specific declarations of the New Testament; it is, in fact, to fail to grasp the implications of its general teaching on the subject. The work of Christ is presented by its apostolic interpreters in terms which specify it,

> a sacrifice for sin, and not a sacrifice in any vague sense. Its value is that it somehow or other neutralises sin as a power estranging man and God, and that in virtue of it God and man are reconciled.[6]

Sacrifice in Israel

In Jewish religion thought, in the context of which Christ's work had its first interpretation (cf. John 4:22), the atoning significance of sacrifice was a commonplace. And it received its further elaboration by the apostolic writers both in specific statement and by contrast with the ancient Levitical rituals. It would seem, therefore, that a reference back to the religious significance of the early sacrificial system must shed some light on the atoning sacrifice of the death of Christ. It is to be accepted, nevertheless, that a biblically acceptable doctrine of Christ's atoning work does not require that the atoning death of Christ be made to fit in with the minutiae of the sacrificial rites of the old economy. For it is, after all, in contrast with the deficiencies and inadequacies of that system that the Epistle to the Hebrews presents the fullness and finality of Christ's work.

The sacrifices of the ancient ritual were prescribed by the law, and their presentation was, for the most part, a matter of obedience to the law. And, even in those sacrifices which some may have regarded as having propitiatory power, there was little, if any, understanding of the nature of sacrifice or of the way it took effect. So is it that the sacrifices of the Old Testament do not cover in analogy the whole of Christ's saving work. Yet the general principles governing such sacrifices must illuminate in some measure the New Testament presentation of Christ's sacrificial work. It is not the case that Jesus nowhere made explicit reference to the sacrificial nature of his death (cf. Matt. 20:28; 26:28), nor that his disciples could have had no understanding of if in such terms. The original disciples were, after all, Israelites indeed, and Paul, a Hebrew of the Hebrews. They were all well versed in the Old Testament, and had read there clearly enough that sacrifices and forgiveness, death and atonement, were linked. And they knew, too, that, whatever other function the various sacrifices fulfilled in their Levitical usage, they did finally have some expiatory significance. The entire ancient ritual was shot through with the thought of sacrifice and affirmed on the principle that it is the blood that makes an atonement for the soul. The whole system was built up to make explicit the necessity of sacrifice for the expiation of sin. Although these sacrifices provided no atonement for wilful transgression and had effect only within the covenant, they did bring to the foreground God's purpose of salvation and manifest the way of its operation.

Interest in the place and purpose of sacrifice in the religious ritual of Israel was heightened by the publication of J. Wellhausen's *Prolegomena of the History of Israel* in 1885 and of W.R. Smith's *The Religion of the Semites* in 1894. Under the notion of the principle of religious development, they both advanced the thesis that the sacrificial system had its origin, for the most part, outside Israel, among people to whom it was of the nature of a celebration in the midst of a sort of semi-religious jamboree. From this lighthearted beginning, they assert, it was introduced into Judaism, to develop by the time of the post-exilic period into the more solemn sin and guilt sacrifices of the Levitical system. It can, indeed, be accepted that sacrifice did not originate with Israel. There are earlier references to sacrifice even within scripture itself, in, for example, the stories of Abel (Gen. 4:4; cf. Heb. 11:4) and of Noah (Gen. 8:20). And Abraham, too, offered sacrifices to God (cf. Gen. 22:3,13 etc.). At the time of Israel's constitution as a nation altars, sacrifices and officiating priests existed among peoples outside Israel as a sort of 'thank you' gift to the deity for the bounties of nature. It may even be that the more spiritually sensitive among them had an awareness of wrongdoing in the light of the law written on their hearts (Rom. 2:15) and a hope that the offering of such sacrifices would make the deity favourable to those who presented them. These ideas about sacrifice can be accepted; but what cannot be accepted, because neither credible nor true, is that the sacrifices of the Levitical code originated in the post-exilic period as a development within Israel from pagan and virtually non-religious beginnings. Rather was the Levitical sacrificial system an element in God's preparatory revelation introduced at the beginning of Israel's history. It indicated the need and nature of sacrifice to bring about the reconciliation of God and man and it would have its complete enactment in the sacrifice of the death of Christ.

While, then, it may be that the Levitical sacrifices 'had a common origin in God's revelation to our earlier ancestors', it is still 'more consonant with a recognition of the special status of Scripture to say that the Israelites (despite their backslidings) preserved the substance of God's original purpose, whereas pagan sacrifices were degenerate corruptions of it.'[7] In Israel the whole focus on and directions for the place of sacrifice in the cultus was of God's institution and requirement.

The sacrifices in the Old Testament were offered on a variety of occasions and for a wide variety of conditions. There are, however, two types of sacrifice which are of special significance for us because of their relation to the sacrificial action of Christ's death. The first of these, the burnt offering is particularly associated with man's creaturely relation to God (cf. Lev. 9;12; Exod. 29:14,17). In the sin and guilt offerings, however, the need of atonement in view of man's sin and guilt was explicitly recognised. The association between the burnt and sin offerings has been stated by van Gemeren like this: 'before the worshipper can fully devote himself to the Lord (symbolised by the burnt offering), he must know that his sins have been atoned for (symbolised by the sin offering).'[8] A.F. Rainey states it more succinctly, 'The burnt-offering, signifying complete surrender to God, was therefore associated with the sin-offering in the process of atonement.'[9] Stott, follows the suggestion of Warfield, that in the burnt offering 'man [is] conceived as creature', while the sin offering has to do with 'the needs of man as sinner'. Thus the former is associated with man as a human being, 'a creature claiming protection', and the latter with the same human being as 'a sinner craving pardon.'[10] Accepting this distinction between the two offerings Stott then makes the important comment:

> Then God is revealed in the sacrifices on the one hand as the Creator on whom man depends for his physical life, and on the other as simultaneously the Judge who demands and the Saviour who provides atonement for sin. Of these two kinds of sacrifice it was further recognised that the latter is the foundation of the former, in that reconciliation to the Judge is necessary before worship of our Creator.[11]

From what has been said it will be clear that the chief feature of the Levitical system was the great importance attached to particular sacrifices, namely the guilt, sin and trespass offerings. They all belong to the expiatory type which was regarded as embodying, more graphically through their vicarious character, the sacrificial idea. And while not connected with any particular transgression their primary reference was to God. They were the means whereby a sinful people could approach the Holy One. Essential to their efficacy was the shedding and sprinkling of blood and the conveyance of the sacrifice entire to God. The blood was for God by necessity and right. Before God the blood had a mysterious potency for sin's atonement. In this way was made actual the Levitical connotation of the use of the word for sacrifice, 'that which is brought near', to secure reconciliation between God and man. Such a thought must have been in Paul's mind when he affirmed to the Ephesians, 'But now in Christ Jesus you who once were far off have been brought near by the blood of Christ' (2:13).

Jesus recognised the authority and significance of the sacrificial law. He kept the Passover and worshipped in the Temple. And he declared the sacrificial purport of his death in reference to the covenant sacrifice with which the Mosaic system was instituted (Matt. 26:28; Luke 22:20; cf. 1 Cor. 11:25). Thus is Christ's death an atoning sacrifice: a sacrifice to secure God's reconciliation to man and an atonement to provide man's redemption by God and for God.

Considering these sacrificial offerings of the old economy, there are to be observed two principles or presuppositions which underlie their use and which have their absolute application to Christ's work. On the one hand, the offerings of sacrifice were for God as the means of man's reconciliation: and, on the other hand, the sacrifice of the offerings was effectual before God as the way of atonement by God for man's sin.

Whatever view may be held concerning the primeval origin of sacrifices, of their divine institution as regards Israel there can be no two opinions. It was by God and for God that the sacrificial system found spiritual and prophetic significance. Likewise, but more emphatically, in the New Testament, is the atonement of Christ's sacrifice set forth as a divine work. It is God himself who made reconciliation by the death of his Son.

A sacrifice was sacrifice offered to God, and, whatever its value, it has that value for him. No one ever thought of offering sacrifice for the sake of a moral effect it was to produce on himself. If we say that the death of Christ was an atoning sacrifice, then, the sacrifice must be an objective atonement. It is to God it is offered, and it is to God it makes a difference. Whatever objections may present themselves to it on reflection, this point of view was universal in the ancient church. The death of Christ was an atoning sacrifice through which sin is annulled and God and man reconciled.[12]

This declaration is no more or less than the apprehension of the significance of the Calvary event for the apostle Paul when he states, 'God presented him [Jesus Christ] as a sacrifice of atonement through faith in his blood' (Rom. 3:25 NIV).

In the person of Christ God has given himself to us; and in the work of Christ the Son of God has given himself for us. Thus is it that the redemption of man in the atonement of the death of Christ is a reality 'affecting Godhead'. To be saved by the redeeming energy of the Calvary event is to know the salvation of God. The atonement of Christ's sacrificial deed is the way, and the place, where God himself has come to man in reconciliation. Thus does Brunner state,

> God alone can make this sacrifice. He alone can expiate, can 'cover' guilt as though it hath never been; he alone can stop up the hole, fill up the trench; for there is something infinite about sin. Over and over again it seems to be forgotten that it is God himself who expiates, who provides the sacrifice.[13]

In the act of expiation God himself does something, he takes the burden upon himself. In the Calvary event God was in some real way present to give something of himself for our sakes. That is the sublime 'transaction' of the cross; the final mystery of the atonement. He who was of God gave himself as 'a fragrant offering and sacrifice to God' (Eph. 5:2), 'in his body of his flesh by his death' (Col. 1:22; cf. Heb. 10:5,10).

There is, then, to be stressed the other issue, that the sacrifice of the offerings were effectual before God as the way of atonement for man's sin. It is to be accepted that in general the sacrifices of the Old Testament had relation to sin; but specifically, in the sin and guilt offerings, is this connection declared. It is not necessary here to adduce a long catena of verses to confirm this statement. The fact of the connection between sin and sacrifice is present in the very terms themselves as it is all-pervasive in the Levitical account. Again and again is there reference to sacrifice as an atonement for sin (Lev. 4:3,14,26,28,35 etc.) Inherent in the word *chattath*, 'sin -offering' are the reality of sin and the mode of its expiation. In spite of the misuse of the system of sacrifice and the antinomian excesses to which it led and against which the prophets vigorously protested, James Denney truly asserts. 'In all probability, by the first century of the Christian era, all sacrifices among the Jews had this character of being expiatory or propitiatory sacrifices; whatever the *modus*, the effect was that they purged or took away sin.'[14] Instinctively, therefore, would the New Testament Christians see in Christ as God's gift to the world a sacrifice for the putting away of sin.

The Sacrifice of Christ

This relationship between Christ's giving of himself and his being a sacrifice for sin pervades the New Testament. The Lord Jesus Christ 'gave himself for our sins' (Gal. 1:4). 'He has now appeared once for all at the end of the age to put away sin by the sacrifice of himself' (Heb. 9:26). He 'through the eternal Spirit offered himself without blemish to God' (Heb. 9:14) that by 'his blood' he would sanctify and cleanse (Heb. 9:13, 14). 'Christ was sacrificed once to take away the sins of many people' (Heb. 9:28 NIV). So in the Calvary event was Christ's sacrifice for sin transacted and the atonement for sin completed. All, all is finished now (cf. Heb. 10:12). The work is done; God and man are reconciled.

Not only did the sacrificial system of the ancient ritual provide the Christians of the first century with a context to apprehend Christ's salvific deed for them, but it was also available to the inspired writers of the New Testament in their effort to interpret more precisely and cogently the Calvary event. In a general sense, it was for them typical of Christ's perfect offering of himself. In its different elements they discerned suggestive correspondences to Christ's sacrifice for human sinfulness. These correspondences they saw in the several sacrifices of the Levitical ritual: in the sin offering (Rom. 8:3; Heb. 13:11; 1 Pet. 3:18); the Passover (1 Cor. 5:7); the covenant (Heb. 9:15); the Day of Atonement (Heb. 9:12f.) The sacrificial acts of that prior economy were seen to be fulfilled in the Calvary event; in the slaying of the sacrificial lamb (1 Pet. 1:19; Rev. 5:6; 13:8); the sprinkling of the blood in the sin offering (Heb. 9:13f.); the covenant sacrifices (1 Pet. 1:2); the slaying of the victim beyond the city gates (Heb. 13:11). In all this, the one in whom it all took place was Christ, Son of God, Saviour, High Priest of our confession. In him and by him was fulfilled all that was necessary to be done for man's salvation 'according to the scriptures'.

Notes

1. Stewart, James, (1935: reprint 1941) *A Man in Christ*, London. Hodder & Stoughton, 236.
2. *ibid.*
3. *ibid.,* 237.
4. Brunner, Emil, (1934) *The Mediator*, tr. Wyon, O., London, Lutterworth, 477.
5. Warfield, B.B., (1920) *Christian Doctrines*, New York, OUP. 435.
6. Denney, James, (1911) *The Christian Doctrine of Reconciliation*, London, Hodder & Stoughton, 29.
7. Stott, John, *The Cross of Christ*, Leicester, Inter-Varsity Press. 135.
8. van Gemeren, W.A., 'Offering and Sacrifices in Bible Times'. in Ewell, W.A. (ed.) *The Evangelical Dictionary of Theology*, Grand Rapids. Baker, 791.
9. Rainey, A.F., (1975) 'Sacrifice and Offerings', in Tenney, M. C. (ed.)*Zondervan Pictorial Encyclopedia of the Bible*, Grand Rapids, Zondervans. 2025,2026.
10. Stott, *op. cit.*, 135,136: cf. Warfield, *op. cit.*, 401-435.
11. Stott, *op. cit.*, 136.
12. Denney, *op. cit.*, 30.
13. Brunner, *op. cit.*, 482.
14. Denney, *op. cit.*, 29.

Chapter XI
A RANSOM PAID

In the two places where the word 'ransom' appears in the New Testament, Matthew 20:28 and 1 Timothy 2:6, it is present as a specific concept to indicate the redemptive significance of the Calvary event. The prefix in its use in the Greek of 1 Timothy 2:6 - *antilutron*- must be taken as giving force to the substitutionary idea, which underlies virtually every other New Testament statement of the atoning purport of Christ's death. Derivative forms of the term *lutron* in the New Testament strengthen the cogency of the ransom concept to express this significance. In these passages the English versions usually translate the noun *lutron* and its strengthened form *apolutrosis* as 'redemption' (Luke 1:68; 2:38; Rom. 3:24; 8:23; 1 Cor. 1:30; Eph. 1:14; 4:30; Heb. 9:12); and such redemption is related to Christ's shed blood (Eph. 1:7; cf. Rev. 5:9 RSV). In Luke 24:21, Titus 2:14 and 1 Peter 1:18, the verbal form used has a corresponding English verbal one in which the redemptive concept is present (cf. AV and NIV). In these verses the RSV follows the AV except in the one instance of 1 Peter 1:18 where it has 'were ransomed'. The Greek word *agorazo* is rendered in the RSV 'didst ransom' in Revelation 5:9, 'for thou wast slain, and by thy blood didst ransom men for God'. In two other instances of its use (Rev. 14:3,4) it retains with the AV the translation 'were redeemed'.

While, however, these cross translations between the terms 'ransom' and 'redeemed' are legitimate, it is nevertheless important to give *lutron* in Matthew 20:28 and *antilutron* in 1 Timothy 2:6 their distinctive connotation as an interpretation of Christ's work. For, as John Stott well observes, quoting Leon Morris, the former word specifically refers to 'a process involving release by payment of a ransom price' which is not necessarily so of the latter.[1] And, continues Stott, 'we have no liberty to dilute its meaning into a vague and cheap deliverance. We have been 'ransomed' by Christ, not merely 'redeemed' or 'delivered' by him'.[2] The exact meaning of the biblical term 'ransom' is given by David Hill, after an intensive linguistic study. He says,' "A ransom is 'paid to gain freedom', or is 'the means by which release is achieved" '.[3]

That Matthew 20:28 is Christ's own declaration of the expiatory value of his death must be allowed. There is no good reason to call its authenticity into question.

The passage more than any other in the synoptic Gospels reveals Jesus' own conviction about his death. In classical usage the term ransom *lutron* was uniformly applied to expiatory sacrifices, and that is the idea here. A ransom is not needed at all except where life has been forfeited. What Christ is saying, then, is that the forfeited lives of men are ransomed by his own life of self surrender in death. The declaration means 'that the many lives are forfeit and that his life is not, so that surrender of his life means liberation of theirs'.[4]

The idea of Christ's death as the ransom price for man's redemption was a familiar interpretation of his reconciling work in the early church. But it led in post-apostolic times to such questions as to whom was the ransom paid - to God or the devil - which produced answers that were so simplistic and crude that the ransom concept was later discarded as neither a reasonable nor right model for Christ's work.

In more recent days, however, under the impact of a renewed interest in biblical theology, the ransom doctrine has been revisited. An important presupposition of this new approach is that the true significance of a New Testament term can best be uncovered by an examination of its Hebrew use in its translation into the Greek of the LXX. In this regard it is to be noted that the term *lutron* translates three much used Hebrew words. One of these, *hopher*, has the idea of a 'covering', or a 'wiping away', though it was used in a generally accepted moral sense of 'making propitiation'. Because of its sacrificial implication it was favoured by S.R. Driver. Says Driver,

the term hopher has the basic sense of 'a covering' (viz. of an offence), hence of a propitiatory gift, but restricted by the usage to a gift offered to propitiate or satisfy the avenger of blood, and so the satisfaction for a life, i.e. a ransom.[5]

For support of this view reference is made to Exodus 21:30; Job 33:24; Isaiah 43:3; Psalm 49:7; Proverbs 6:35. The validity of this pedigree is, however, rendered less acceptable by the observation of James Orr, 'that in all this range of meaning the word 'ransom' is never in the Old Testament directly connected with propitiatory sacrifice.'[6]

Supporters of an alternative view appeal to the Hebrew words *goel* and *padah*, each of which carries the thought of 'liberation'. Behind their use, it is contended, stands the obligation to redeem that rests upon the kinsman, the *goel* of Leviticus 25:51. In the LXX *goel* is here translated *lutron*, while in the verse itself the fact of a ransom price is specifically stated. Confirmation of this background of ideas in which that of ransom features in the rendering of *padah* is sustained by reference to Psalm 69:18 (also Isa. 35:10; 51:11; Jer. 31:11; Hos. 13:14); as is that of *goel* in Isaiah 51:10 and Jeremiah 31:11.

James Denney prefers to follow the suggestion of Ritschl and take Psalm 49:7f. and Job 33:23f. as the more probable Old Testament passages to furnish a clue to our Lord's meaning regarding the ransoming efficacy of his life surrendered to the death of the cross.[7] The Psalmist confesses man's inability to ransom himself or give to God an acceptable price for his life. Such a ransom price he deems too 'costly, and can never suffice' (Ps.49: 7-8). And Job, too, sees a man - himself certainly - 'chastened' and 'wasted', looking for a 'mediator', an 'angel perchance to spare him from 'going down to the pit' (Job 33:24). If such a mediator could be found he would announce to the man, 'I have found a ransom' for him. But neither the Psalmist nor Job can provide a ransom that would meet their case. Only in God, they conclude, can such be found. So the Psalmist declares, 'But God will ransom my soul from the power of Sheol, for he will receive me' (Ps.49:15). And likewise, Job tells the man who could not find for himself a ransom to pray to God and he will accept him (Job 33:26) and, acknowledging his sin, he will discover and testify that in his life shall he 'see the light' (v. 28).

In Denney's opinion, and in ours, it seems hardly open to doubt that the climate of thought in our Lord's mind as he uttered the words of Matthew 20:28 was that of Psalm 49, with a glance also at Job 33. The Psalmist is aware of the costly nature of any such acceptable ransom; so costly indeed, that the man himself cannot fulfil its measure. Both the Psalmist and Job confess that it belongs to God himself to ransom and redeem. These facts are most surely to be underscored in the interpretation of Matthew 20:28 and 1 Timothy 2:6. It is not of man to ransom and redeem himself. Salvation is of God; in the whole plan and provision of it. It is God who provides the ransom and accepts it. 'God sent forth his Son' for this intent; and he, the Son of man, came not to be served but to serve and give his life a ransom for many. Such is God's ransom, costly beyond human reckoning; and such a ransom did 'suffice' in superabundant measure for man's redemption. It is, consequently,

> true to experience to say that man's emancipation from evil cost Christ dear. It is true to the most elementary forms of Christian experience to say that he gave himself a ransom for us. It is also true to say that he had to do it. In the work of man's deliverance from sin and reconciliation to God, we are in contact with moral necessities which cannot be ignored and which make the task of our delivery costly and severe .... We are not bought for nothing, we are bought with a price. Our redemption was conditioned by the recognition of moral necessities which had to be recognised, and the recognition of which involved the death of Jesus on the cross.[8]

In saying that he gave 'his life a ransom' Christ was certainly focusing man's redemption on the Calvary event. The giving of his life has no other meaning than that he gave himself unto death. And in that death is our soul's ransom (Rom. 5:6,8; 6:10; 1 Cor. 15:3 etc.); and in the blood of the cross man's redemption (Eph. 1:7; Col. 1:14; 1 Pet. 1:18; cf. Rom. 3:24-25; Acts 20:28). We are thus bought with a price (1 Cor. 6:20; 7:23), to a redemption which moves us to glorify God and enjoy his favour.

In the words 'a ransom for many' there is implied man's condition of need. For Christ saw mankind held in captivity to sin, death and the devil; held in a captivity so real and tyrannising that only a ransom of such cost as he, the Son of God, could himself alone pay would suffice for his liberation.

There was no other good enough,
To pay the price of sin.

Such ransom had its effect in Christ's giving of his life to bring about man's redemption. For in the ransom of his death Christ accomplished his mediatory role of reconciling God to man and man to God. In the passage in Job 33 the two concepts mediator and ransom are juxtaposed (v.23-24), so as to indicate a connection between them. Significantly, in the text of 1 Timothy 2:5-6f. they occur in a like relationship: 'For there is one God, and there is one mediator between God and men, the man Christ Jesus, who gave himself as a ransom for all, the testimony to which was borne at the proper time.' Christ's mediatory office has universal actualisation in the giving of himself as a ransom for all. In the Word made flesh the man Jesus Christ provided, in his death, the price of man's reconciliation to God.

In two other places only in the new Testament is the title 'mediator' (*mesites*) applied to our Lord; both are in the Epistle to the Hebrews (Heb. 9:15; 12:24). In Hebrews 8:6, however, his mediatory action is referred to though the title is not used: 'Christ has given a far higher ministry for he mediates a higher agreement, which in turn rests upon higher promises' (Phillips). But while the title 'Mediator' is thus scarce in the New Testament, the idea of persons acting out the role of a mediator permeates the whole of scripture. In the Old Testament it comes to prominence in the sigh of Job: 'there is no umpire [AV 'daysman', LXX *Mesites* - 'middle-man'], between us, who might lay hand upon us both' (Job 9:33). The mediator is one who intervenes between two parties, either in order to make or restore peace and friendship or to ratify a covenant. In the area of human relationships there is the record of Joab who played the mediator's role between David and Absalom (2 Sam. 14:1-23). It is, however, within the sphere of Old Testament religion that the awareness of the need of a mediator and the way of the mediation provided have specific recognition. The Old Testament priest and prophet fulfilled the office of mediator within the terms of God's covenant with man. The prophets spoke for God in the presence of men; and the priests acted for men in the presence of God. But while each fulfilled a mediatory role in the Old Testament economy their functions were alike shadows of the better things to come to fulfilment in the one mediator between God and man, the man Christ Jesus who gave himself a ransom for all. In Galatians 3:19. Moses is understood to act the mediatory role between God and the People in the giving of the law; but his position as mediator is sharply contrasted with Christ (cf. vv. 14,17). Moses was a *mesites* between two contracting parties, God and Israel; but in the case of Christ it is otherwise for 'an intermediary implies more than one; but God is one' (v. 20). In the case of the relationship between God and and man there are not two parties equally seeking reconciliation. It is, of course, a fact that the words of Galatians 3:20 'an intermediary implies more than one; but God is one', are difficult for exegetes to interpret. It is, indeed, said that no other passage of scripture has so exercised the ingenuity of commentators. B. Jowett has computed the number of interpretations to be 430; a total which seems rather excessive, but as he does not chronicle them we have no means of checking. Jowett may have carried over into his count the number of years alluded to in chapter 3:17! Lightfoot, however, is more modest; he gives the number to be between 200 and 300.

In spite of this disheartening fact, however, the drift of Paul's contention seems clear enough. A mediator - and the word in this verse is the same as in the previous one - has the character of a 'middle-man', an intermediary; and between these two parties, the mediator interposes his good offices to bring them together. As observed, the law came through the mediation of Moses: it came thus only indirectly from God. In the giving of God's new covenant, by contrast, no merely human mediator stood between. Thus the words 'but God is one' would seem to indicate one of two things: or, maybe, both together. In contrast with the promulgation of the law with its intermediaries, the promise came directly from God. God is the one, and the only one, who originates and executes it. He, the giver, is everything; the recipients are nothing, for such stand before God under the curse of the law as transgressors. God himself alone is the origin and organ of the promise. But a further and deeper note may underlie the apostle's statement. God is one; the one who acts in the fulfilment of the promise is the 'Seed' spoken of in verse 16. He is no mere human intermediary (cf. 4:4f.) Certainly, he is man's representative and substitute; yet he is one with God. Thus is God himself at once the direct source of the promise and the only mediator of it. Christ includes both parties in his own person. He is in himself both the human embodiment of the promises of God and the divine Son in whom the promises were made actual and available in their fulfilment. It is he who 'hath redeemed us from the curse of the law, being made a curse for us' (3:13 AV). To be thus redeemed is to be ransomed; and he ransomed us by himself becoming 'a curse' for us. He became the very thing the law made us, 'a curse'. So identified was he with us that all we are as sinners became truly and actually his. The law brought us under the 'curse'; but he brought himself under it and made the curse of the law his own. He became what we are in the awfulness of the law's condemnation and judgement of its curse. He experienced in himself all the law's dark threatenings and all of God's wrath upon sin by being himself the object of that condemnation and wrath. He became cursed by the law in holy reprobation for our ransom. This he did 'on our behalf '; fully and finally he bore our sins in his body to the tree. Yet he did 'on our behalf ' this great thing 'for us' because in some real and true sense he did it 'in our place'. He stood where we should have stood, but never could, 'made sin' (2 Cor. 5:21) yet never a sinner, and 'cursed' (Gal. 3:13) yet never himself convicted by the law of any infraction. This is what it means to speak of Christ as 'the one mediator between God and man'.

It is important, therefore, to note that the references to Christ as mediator are immediately connected with his death. He is the mediator who gave himself a ransom for all (1 Tim. 5:6). Christ is presented as 'the mediator' of a new covenant 'by means of death' (Heb. 9:15b AV). In Hebrews 12:24 he is declared to be 'the mediator of a new covenant' ratified by 'the sprinkled blood that speaks more graciously than the blood of Abel' His blood speaks 'more graciously' because it speaks in terms of the grace that saves in contrast with the law that condemns. It is supremely in the giving of himself as a ransom - in his death, his cross, his blood - that the efficacy of his mediation lies. It is, of course, proper to insist that Christ's whole life and ministry should be read in mediatory terms. All through his ministry Jesus fulfilled the function of prophet (cf. Deut. 18:18; Matt. 13:54f.). yet not so much as the prophet *par excellence* as being himself the subject of all prophecy, did he speak for God (cf. John 14:24; 17:14,17). So. too, did he act throughout the days of his flesh to reveal God and thereby demonstrate among men his appointment and anointing as God's Messiah to give his life a ransom for many. All he said and did 'in the flesh' was said and done in the awareness of his filial relationship with the Father which called for the Father's approbation: 'This is my beloved Son in whom I am well pleased'. He lived a life of perfect obedience and so exhibited the reality of a new relationship between God and man achieved for mankind in his mediatory action in the Calvary event. In all that he did in his living among men he revealed God to man for the fulfilment of his messianic purpose. And that fulfilment was consummated, and only could be consummated. in his death.

So is it that in the person of Christ God has given himself to us and in his work Christ has given God to us in a ransom for our redemption; a ransom for our redemption secured not with perishable things as silver and gold but 'with the precious blood of Christ' like that of a lamb without blemish or spot' (1 Pet. 1:19). Because Christ paid the ransom price we have redemption. For such sinners as we all are Christ is the mediator of 'a new' (Heb. 9:15) and 'a better' (Heb. 8:6) covenant established and confirmed in his blood (Heb. 9:14).

> In the sight of God our Saviour . . . who would have all men saved . . . there is only one God, and only one intermediary between God and man, the Man Jesus Christ. He gave himself a ransom for us all - an act of redemption which happened once, but which stands for all time as a witness to what he is (1 Tim. 2:5, 6) (Phillips).

Notes

1. Stott, John, *The Cross of Christ*, Leicester, Inter-Varsity Press. 176: cf. Morris, Leon (1955) *The Apostolic Preaching of the Cross*, London, Tyndale Press, 10; Morris, Leon (1965), *The Atonement: its Meaning and Significance*, London, IVP, 106ff.
2. *ibid*., Stott.
3. Hill,David, (1967)*Greek Words and Hebrew Meanings: Studies in the Semantics of Soteriological Terms*, Cambridge University Press 67f.
4. McDonald, H.D., (1985) 'The Atonement of the Death of Christ', in *Faith, Revelation, and History* Grand Rapids, Baker, 68: cf. Denney, James (1985) *Studies in Theology*, 3rd edn London, Hodder & Stoughton, 133.
5. Driver, S.R., (1906) 'Propitiation', in Hastings, J.(ed) *Dictionary of the Bible*, Edinburgh, T.& T. Clark: iv, 128.
6. Orr, James, (1909) 'Ransom', in Hastings, J.(ed) *Dictionary of Christ and the Gospels*, Edinburgh, T.& T. Clark, ii, 460.
7. Denney, J., (1911) *The Death of Christ*, (rev. edn), London. Hodder & Stoughton 31f.; cf. Ritschl, Albrecht, (1900)*The Christian Doctrine of Justification and Reconciliation: The Positive Development of the Doctrine*, ed. MacKintosh, H.R. and Macauley, A.B. Edinburgh, T. & T. Clark: New York, Scribner, ii, 69f.
8. Denney, J., (1911) *The Christian Doctrine of Reconciliation*. London, Hodder & Stoughton, 32, 33.

Chapter XII
A PROPITIATION OFFERED

On four occasions a form of the Greek word *hilasterion* appears in the New Testament; and in three of these instances the AV translates as 'propitiation' (Rom 3:25 - *hilasterion*; 1 John 2:2; 4:10 - *hilasmos*). The verbal form *hilaskesthai* is rendered 'to make reconciliation' in Hebrews 2:17 in the same version. The basic idea of the term 'propitiation' and, indeed, of 'reconciliation' is that of the pacification of one's wrath or anger by the rendering of an acceptable offering. The word *hilasterion* belongs to a group of Greek adjectives with the termination *-erion* which expresses the thought - 'that which serves an end'. The meaning, therefore, of the term *hilasterion* conveys the idea of an act or attitude of a person which induces one hitherto hostile to show favour or goodwill. It expresses, simply, the turning away of wrath by an offering acceptable to this end. The verb *hilaskesthai* corresponds in the LXX to the Hebrew *kipper* and has the double meaning of 'to pardon' and 'to expiate' both of which ideas are enshrined in the concept of making atonement. The text of Romans 3:25 declares that God himself set forth Christ as a propitiation through faith in his blood whereby to pardon man's sin in righteousness. On the verse Calvin comments:

> I prefer thus literally to retain the language of Paul: for it seems to be that he intended, by one single sentence, to declare that God is propitious to us as soon as we have our trust resting on the blood of Christ.[1]

The Wrath of God

The use of the term 'propitiation', then, which carries the sense of a wrath diverted by means which make the estranged one propitious raises various questions. Can God really be conceived as an offended party? What need of a propitiatory offering to secure his forgiveness? Some modern theologians deny outright that there is such a reality in God as wrath or anger. It is in this conviction, in fact, that the term propitiation has been deleted from some modern translations: on the assumption, that is, that the word presupposes an impossible view of God, as one who can give expression to wrath. Thus the RSV substitutes 'expiation' and the NEB 'the means of expiation' in Romans 3:25; and in Hebrews 2:17 'to expiate the sins', while in 1 John 2:2;

4:10 NEB prefers 'the remedy for the defilement of our sins'. It is argued that by admitting the word 'expiation' or such kindred terms the proper object of God's Calvary action is more correctly focused. For the concept 'propitiation' implies there is wrath to be appeased, but, since wrath has no place in God, the idea of placating God gives a false notion of the divine being. Besides, while propitiation has a Godward reference, that of 'expiation' relates more particularly to human sin and guilt. So Driver boldly declares that it is never implied in the New Testament that 'the offerer of such a sacrifice is outside God's disposition of grace, or the object of his wrath.'[2]

Foremost among those in recent years who have advocated this thesis, and who, indeed, became its leading exponent, is C.H. Dodd. In a comment on 1 John 2:2 he declares the translation 'propitiation' in the text to be 'illegitimate', as it is likewise in its every other instance in the New Testament.[3] And he asserts emphatically elsewhere that, 'Hellenistic Judaism, as represented by the LXX' never regards 'the cultus as a means of pacifying the displeasure of the Deity, but as a means of delivering man from sin.'[4] The basic objection of Dodd and his many contemporary allies and their numerous successors is that such an idea of God is crude and unbiblical; and is inconsistent with the New Testament proclamation that God is love.

But on two counts the thought enshrined in the first of the two questions posed, that the idea of God's wrath is cancelled out by the revelation of God as love, does not hold up. The first is that the biblical revelation itself plainly teaches otherwise. It is not at all true that the Bible knows nothing of a God of wrath. Indeed, as J.I. Packer declares, 'One of the most striking things about the Bible is the vigour with which both Testaments emphasise the reality and terror of God's wrath.'[5] And he quotes with approval the observation of A.W. Pink, 'A study of the Concordance will show that there are more references in Scripture to the anger, fury, and wrath of God, than there are to his love and tenderness.'[6]

It has, indeed, been computed that there are at least 20 different words in the Old Testament to express the divine wrath; and that the Old Testament makes 585 usages of them to declare his righteous anger against the unrighteousness of man. The wrath of God is real. It is no sham; no make-believe. Often in the Old Testament is God's wrath further qualified as 'fierce' (2 Chron. 28:11; 29:10; 30:8 etc.); 'kindled' (Num. 11:1; Deut. 11:17; 2 Kings 22:17; Ps. 2:11 etc.); 'great' (2 Chron. 34:21 etc.); and 'a consuming fire' (Ezek. 21:31). While it is true that the New Testament focuses particularly on the love of God, it does not, nevertheless, give any support to the Marcionite notion that the wrathful God of the Old Testament is another being from the New Testament God of love who holds no resentment against man's wicked ways. The fact of the matter is that there is statement enough in the New Testament to indicate God's wrath against evil; and even that of Christ. As regards the latter, R.V.G. Tasker points out that 'wrath' is attributed to Christ in Mark 3:5, and, if some manuscripts are allowed, also in Mark 1:41.[7] The Book of Revelation speaks of the 'wrath of the Lamb' in the final drama of the divine judgement (cf. 6:16-17), which wrath is associated with that of God, the Almighty (19:15; cf. 11:8; 16:19). The wrath of God is also emphasised in such passages as Rom. 1:18; 2:5; 4:15; 5:9; Eph. 2:3; Col. 3:6; 1 Thess. 1:10; 2:16; 5:9; Heb. 3:11; 4:3.

The other consideration which makes void the contention that wrath is not proper to God derives from God's absolute nature as holy. The wrath of God is not other than his own self-affirmation as infinitely holy against all that is antagonistic to his essential goodness.

Thus is his [God's] holy divine wrath, the negative aspect of the Divine holiness. The divine wrath corresponds to our guilt and sin. Whether man's relation to God is really conceived in personal terms or not is proved by the fact of the recognition of the divine wrath as the objective correlate to human guilt. This, then, is the obstacle which alienates us from God. It is no merely apparent obstacle, no mere misunderstanding: this separation is an objective reality, the twofold reality of human guilt and divine wrath.

It is because God is so near to us that guilt is so terrible. The more sin is acknowledged as sin against God, and so an offence to his holiness, the more serious it becomes and the more irrevocable it is. Since man's attitude towards God has become perverted because of sin, God's attitude towards man has, as a consequence, changed. Both became estranged the one from the other.

It must be clear, then, that to deny the wrath of God is to do violence to the apostolic gospel, and to nullify the verdict of the human sense of guilt. To take seriously the holiness of God is at once to accept the reality of the divine wrath. So does P.T. Forsyth declare that 'Everything begins in our theology with the holiness of God'.[9] The overwhelming reality of God's wrath lays bare the appalling fact of sin against a holy God. And the holiness of God, in its recoil from sin, meets the sinner in judgement. So is the judgement of God altogether just and right. It is not, therefore, without significance that the biblical terms for righteousness and justice overlap in expressing God's essential nature as holy (cf. Deut. 32:4; Isa. 45:21 AV; Zeph. 3:5; Acts 3:14 AV; Rev. 15:3). Thus is the release of God's wrath against sinful humanity a righteous judgement and just punishment.

There is, then, little to be said in favour of the modern denial of God's wrath in his righteous reaction against sin. C.H. Dodd insists that what is termed the divine wrath is to be understood as the operation of impersonal forces in the natural and moral order; a sort of cause-effect reaction in nature. He declares that, increasingly with the development of the religious understanding of God's way with his world, the Old Testament writers came more and more to conceive of 'punishment' for evil done, in an 'impersonal manner'. Stating this as an established fact, A.T. Hanson goes on to affirm that the apostle Paul likewise held the same view. He writes:

> there can be little doubt that for Paul the impersonal character of the wrath was important; it relieved him of the necessity of attributing wrath directly to God, it transformed the wrath from an attribute to God into a name for a process, which sinners bring upon themselves.[10]

Since, then, for Dodd and Hanson what is referred to as 'the wrath of God' is 'wholly impersonal', it follows that any idea of the work of Christ in terms of 'propitiation' becomes sheer nonsense. Hanson is no less emphatic in this regard than Dodd, 'If we think of the wrath as an attitude of God', he writes, 'you cannot avoid some theory of propitiation. But the wrath in the New Testament is never spoken of as being propitiated, because it is not conceived of as being an attitude of God.'[11] The phrase 'there can be little doubt' in the earlier quotation from Hanson is a dubious expedient designed to suggest that there is no other interpretation credible. But the fact is that it is the alternative that is most surely right. The major premise of his second declaration, namely, that wrath has no place in God, is false, so his conclusion, that there is no need of propitiation, is unwarranted.

Wrath truly is an attribute and attitude of God in relation to sin and a necessary action of his being as absolutely holy. Therefore, the idea of propitiation as an appeasing of his wrath is an admissible concept. Commenting on the term propitiation in Romans 3:25, Frederic Platt insists:

> Its interpretation as 'a propitiatory sacrifice' - a means of rendering God consistently favourable towards sinful men and the means of reconciliation between God and man - is the most natural and, indeed, the only meaning suitable to the context of Rom. 3:25: other Pauline passages harmonise with it better than any other (cf. Rom. 5:9; 6:20; 7:23; Gal. 3:13; 6:9).[12]

Paul Tillich would reject the understanding of propitiation as God's way of bringing about reconciliation of man to himself by dismissing God's wrath and condemnation as mere symbols of man's experience of despair, arising out of his estrangement from the Ground of his Being and his condition of finitude. For him, since God is hardly personal, the idea of a wrath of God issuing forth in judgement is without meaning. He therefore speaks of an 'immanent judgement always going on in history even where the name of Jesus is not known but where the power of the New Being, which is his being, is present or absent.'[13]

Tillich has consequently no place for the propitiatory nature of Christ's work. He allows, to be sure, that 'God participates in the suffering of existential estrangement', but he adds immediately that 'his suffering is not a substitute for the suffering of the creature . . . No substitution but free participation is the necessity of the divine suffering.'[14] It is not necessary to comment on this strange view of Tillich, except to note that with him, too, as with Dodd and Hanson, denial of the wrath of a personal God means the refusal to admit the propitiatory nature of the Calvary event. However, as Denney observes, the 'propitiation is the recognition of what sin is to God, in all its solemn reality.'[15] Only in relation to God, and in the acknowledgement of the justice of his wrath can the concept of propitiation have meaning.

The Love of God

The other issue, derived from the second question posed on above, objecting to the interpretation of the work of Christ in terms of propitiation as the appeasing of God's wrath, is the contention that such an idea is at odds with his love. Since God is revealed as love, the argument runs, there is no need of a propitiation. The answer to this lies in Paul's statement in Romans 3:25. Paul emphasises that it is God himself who sets forth Christ, the Son of his love, as the means of propitiation through his blood. The propitiation is of God's own providing. In 1 John 4:10 this propitiation is related to his love; he loved, us, and sent his Son to be the propitiation for our sins. Such is the divine love. The propitiation is contained in his love. It is God's righteous wrath that necessitated the propitiation; it is God's love that provided the means. In the event of Calvary God's love for the sinner and God's judgement on sin unite for man's redemption. The surest evidence for his love is there. It is not right, therefore, to oppose the love of God to his requirement of a propitiation and to argue that because God is love there is no necessity for such. The truth is quite other. It is just because God is love that he has himself put forth an acceptable propitiatory sacrifice, whereby man is reconciled to him and he to them in righteousness. 'God shows his love for us in that while we were yet sinners Christ died for us' (Rom. 5:8). Equally expressed, then, in the propitiatory sacrifice of the cross are God's holiness and love; his judgement and compassion. God would not be true to himself if he did not judge sin in wrath, nor would he be true to himself if he did not redeem sinners in love. 'To put it in a word, it is in Christ as *hilasterion* that justice is done, not only to the grace of God but to his wrath.'[16]

The wrath of God disclosed how seriously God regards sin. It is under his condemnation. What was overcome in Christ's propitiatory sacrifice born out of God's love was not just man's distrust of God, but God's righteous condemnation of sinful man. It is this special character of sin, its drawing forth from God of his wrath and condemnation, with which Christ deals. He dealt with it by submitting, in his death, to God's judgement thereon as the expression of his righteousness. The fact that God himself met in the death of Christ the requirement of his holy judgement on sin is the final manifestation of his love. 'The propitiatory death of Christ, as an all-transcending demonstration of love, evokes in sinful souls a response which is the whole of Christianity.'[17]

Every instance of the use of the term *hilasterion*, and their united witness, brings out the truth that Christ, by the offering of his blood in his death, fulfilled a function analagous to, but infinitely transcending, that to which the term 'propitiation' was applied in the Old Testament. In Romans 3:25 Paul makes clear that he regards 'propitiation', in its proper meaning as essential to the disclosure of God's nature in its aspect of righteousness and love. It is no arbitrary arrangement depending simply on God's good pleasure. Such propitiation is a natural and moral necessity of God's fundamental being, to demonstrate his righteousness. The Johannine passage gives a more personal reference to the propitiation. For John the propitiation is inseparably associated with the person of Jesus Christ, the righteous (1 John 2:1), as if to imply that the righteous nature of God requires a righteous order of redemption. The declaration is specific that Christ himself is the propitiatory sacrifice 'not for ours only: but also for the sins of the whole world.' It affirms that there is an objective accomplishment, a finished work, as the source from which individual forgiveness and cleansing from sin proceed. 'He is the propitiation' (1 John 2:2 AV), and 'the blood of Jesus cleanses us from all sin' (1 John 1:7).

Astonishingly, Barth, in his comment on Romans 3:25, adopts the opinion first apparently advanced by Origen and affirmed by Ritschl among others, that *hilasterion* signifies 'the mercy seat', or, even more specifically, 'the lid of the ark' of Hebrews 9:5. The idea is not much favoured by modern commentators, and in the light of Godet's arguments the idea would seem impossible to sustain. Therefore, the term *hilasterion*, in its specific meaning as a propitiatory sacrifice, a means of turning aside the wrath of God, must be allowed. Such is the condition of reconciliation brought about in man's relation to God by the Calvary event. For God himself presented Christ as a sacrifice of atonement through faith in his blood. He did this to demonstrate his justice, because in his divine forbearance he had passed over former sins; it was to prove, at the present time, that he himself is righteous and that he justifies him who has faith in Jesus' (Rom. 3:25-26).

The propitiation demonstrates God's righteousness; and his righteousness is made actual in the propitiation. Thus does Calvin comment on the verse of Romans (3:25) 'there is not probably in the whole Bible a passage which sets forth more profoundly the righteousness of God in Christ.'[19] And Barth, too, although he has somewhat weakened the declaration by adopting the 'mercy seat' interpretation, can yet affirm the essential significance of the passage as a true propitiation. He writes:

> The propitiation occurs at the place of the propitiation - only by blood, whereby we are solemnly reminded that God gives life only through death. Consequently, in Jesus also atonement occurs only through the faithfulness of God, by his blood; only, that is to say, in the inferno of his complete solidarity with the sin and weakness and misery of the flesh; in the secret of an occurrence - hero, prophet, wonder-worker - which mark the brilliance of human life, a brilliance which shone also in his life, whilst he lived a man among men; and, finally, in the absolute scandal of his death upon the cross. By the blood Jesus is proved to be the Christ, the first and last Word to men of the faithfulness of God. By his death he declares the impossible possibility of our redemption, and shows himself as the light from uncreated, as the Herald of the Kingdom of God. 'In the picture of the Redeemer, the dominant colour is blood' (Ph. Fr. Hiller), because, in the way of the Cross, in the offering of his life, and in his death, the radical nature of the redemption which he brings and the utter novelty of the word which he proclaims are first brought to light.[20]

The Psalmist poses the questions, 'Has God forgotten to be gracious? Has he in anger shut up his compassion?' (Ps. 77:9). It is not recorded what answer the Psalmist returned to his own question. But Paul has the answer for us. God did not shut up his compassion; for he has provided himself a propitiation - Christ, who in his blood bore the punishment of our sin and the shame of our guilt. In wrath God has remembered grace. In the Calvary event his love broke through his wrath and his holiness found satisfaction in the *hilasterion* - the propitiation - for our sins which his love provided.

Notes

1. Calvin. J.,*Commentaries on the Epistle of Paul to the Romans*. tr. and ed. (1947) Owen, John, Grand Rapids, Eerdmans

2. Driver, S.R., (1946) 'Propitiation' in Hastings, J. (ed.), *Dictionary of the Bible*, Edinburgh, T.& T. Clark, iv. 131.

3. Dodd, C.H., (1946) *The Johnannine Epistles, The Moffatt New Testament Commentary*. London, Hodder & Stoughton; (1935) *The Epistle of Paul to the*

Romans, London, Hodder & Stoughton.
4. Dodd, C.H., (1935) *The Bible of the Greeks*, London, Hodder & Stoughton, 93.
5. Packer, J.I., (1973)*Knowing God*, London, Hodder & Stoughton. 164,165.
6. *ibid.*, cf. Pink, A.W., *The Attributes of God*, Cleveland, Bible Truth, 75.
7. Tasker, R.V.G., (1951) *The Biblical Doctrine of the Wrath of God*, London, Tyndale Press, vii.
8. Brunner, E., (1934) *The Mediator*, tr. Wyon, O. London, Lutterworth, 465.
9. Forsyth, P.T., *The Work of Christ*, London, Hodder & Stoughton. 78.
10. Hanson, A.T., (1959) *The Wrath of the Lamb*, London, SPCK, 110.
11. *ibid.*, 192.
12. Platt, F., (1915) 'Propitiation' *Dictionary of the Apostolic Church.* Edinburgh, T.& T. Clark, ii, 283.
13. Tillich, Paul, (1951-63) *Systematic Theology*, Chicago, University of Chicago Press; London, Nisbet, iii, 189.
14. *ibid.*, ii, 203.
15. Denney, James, (1911) *The Christian Doctrine of Reconciliation*, London, Hodder & Stoughton, 162.
16. *ibid.*, 161.
17. Denney, James, (1911) *The Death of Christ*, (rev.edn), London, Hodder & Stoughton, 128.
18. Godet, F., (1883)*Commentary on Romans*, Edinburgh, T. & T. Clark, 254,255.
19. *ibid.*, Calvin.
20. Barth, Karl, (1933) *The Epistle to the Romans* tr. Hoskyns, Edwyn C. (1933), Oxford, OUP, 105,106.

Chapter XIII
A RECONCILIATION EFFECTED

The basic idea in the Greek term *katallage* is that of the exchange of coins of equivalent value. This significance of the word was common among ancient Greek writers. Thus the idea of 'exchange' is inherent in the word itself. From this basic notion there developed the meaning the term has in the New Testament. The idea developed from that of the exchange of sympathy, understanding and confidence to that of reconciliation in personal relations. But in this context there is present the implication that a prior hostility existed in the heart and mind, usually of both (but sometimes of one) parties, which has been or needs to be allayed before friendship could be restored. In its religious use in the Pauline letters the word denotes the change of relationship between God and man from one of enmity due to man's sin to that of acceptance by and friendship with God, brought about by means of Christ's atoning action in the Calvary event.

To modern theologians the idea of reconciliation as a redemptive term has special appeal, because it interprets the atonement in more personal terms than propitiation. There are, indeed, a number of allied words and phrases which also focus this personal thought. In the actuality of the Calvary event man is brought near to God (Eph. 2:13) through Christ 'making peace' (Col. 1:20, cf. Acts 10:36; Eph. 2:17), so that man may have ˙peace with God' (Rom. 5:1). There is, however, a certain connectedness between the two terms 'reconciliation' and 'propitiation'. For whereas reconciliation presents an atone-ment as a result of atonement, propitiation secures that atonement and brings about the reconciliation. Reconciliation, that is to say, makes past propitiation an ever-present reality in God's reconciled personal relationship with man. Thus in Hebrews 2:17, the AV reads, 'to make reconciliation for the sins of the people' where the Greek text has *hilaskesthai* which, the 1881 RV renders 'to make propitiation' and the NIV 'to make atonement'.

The Old Testament pedigree of the verb 'to reconcile' is slender and has little illumination to bring to its New Testament usage. The Hebrew word occurs in Leviticus 6:30; 8:15; 16:30 and Ezekiel 45:15,17,20 where the EVV translate 'to make atonement'. The only two references in the Old Testament which have any bearing on its use in the New Testament are 2

Chronicles 29:24 and Daniel 9:24. In 2 Chronicles 29:24 priests present the blood of slaughtered goats on the altar and so 'make an atonement for all Israel' (AV). The RSV translation is, to make 'a sin offering with their blood on the altar, to make atonement for all Israel'. In both translations an identity is made between reconciliation and atonement. It is in the atonement that reconciliation is accomplished. So it is in Daniel 9:24 where there is reference to making 'an end of sins, and to make reconciliation ['to atone' RSV, NIV] for iniquity, and to bring in everlasting righteousness' (AV). James Orr is however, right to point out that these Old Testament examples have only an indirect bearing on the New Testament word *katallage*, the idea of which is not propitiation but a change from variance into one of fellowship.'[1]

Although the term is absent from the Gospels, except in the relationship between individuals (cf. Matt. 5:24), yet the reality of reconciliation pervades the whole ministry of Christ. And, throughout, its two-way character is implied. Its Godward side is present in Christ's exercise of divine forgiveness as the supreme blessing of the Kingdom of God which he came to inaugurate (cf. Matt. 6:12,14,15). It is further implied in Christ's whole saving and healing ministry (cf. Matt. 18:10-14; Luke 4:17-21). His every act of mercy and of compassion was a revelation of the Father's willingness to be reconciled to man (cf. Matt. 11:28-29; Luke 15:12ff.). On the human side it is necessary for people to repent to experience the reconciliation (Matt. 4:17; Mark 1:15 etc.) and to respond to Christ's invitation (Matt. 11:28) that they might be renewed to sonship in the kingdom (Matt. 5:9,48; Luke 6:35-36). As sons of God, it is theirs to trust the Father (Matt. 6:24f.) and do his will (Matt. 5:48; 7:21f. etc.)

Denney can therefore declare with reference to Christ's ministry,
'in the widest sense, it will not be questioned, that it was a work of reconciliation. He received sinners. He declared, bestowed, and embodied forgiveness. He came to seek and to save that which was lost. Whatever else he did, he came to men who were alienated from God by their sins, full of apprehension and distrust, and brought them back to God and to the assurance of his fatherly love. That was the general character and result of his life's work in relation to individuals . . . We may say that the reconciling virtue of his being was centred in his death, or that the reconciling virtue of his death pervaded his being; in any case, that the whole influence exerted upon sinners by Jesus is an influence by which, through penitence and faith, they are won from sin to God - in other words is a reconciling influence - cannot be denied.'[2]
If, then, Paul makes reconciliation dependent on Christ's person and his

atoning death, it is no less evident that in the Gospels Christ himself viewed the whole purpose of his coming in the foretold messianic salvation, and on occasions specifically connected it with his death (Matt. 20:28; Luke 24:46-47; cf. John 3:14-15). The apostle Paul alone of the New Testament writers uses the concept 'reconciliation' of the relation brought about between God and man in the Calvary event. 'To reconcile' is an act of God; 'to be reconciled' is the result for man. On three occasions, Paul has the noun *katallage* 'reconciliation' (Rom. 11:15; 2 Cor. 5:18, 19; cf. Heb. 2:17 where the verb *hilaskesthai* is rendered in the KJV, 'to make reconciliation'). In each case it denotes God's action. The apostle regards it as his 'ministry' (2 Cor. 5:18), and 'message' (2 Cor. 5:19) to urge men 'to be reconciled to God' (2 Cor. 5:20). He would bring man into relationship with God's action in the Calvary event as reconciling the world to himself (2 Cor. 5:19).

Mutual Reconciliation?

There are two questions posed in relation to the issue of reconciliation which call for consideration. The first of these is: is the reconciliation mutual? Hesitancy with regard to the Godward side of reconciliation, which necessitates a change in God's attitude towards sinners from wrath to friendship, arises from two sources. On the one hand, as we have seen in the case of propitiation, it is because of the idea of God's wrath and God's love are set in opposition as being mutually exclusive; and, on the other hand, because the concept of a 'change' in God is questioned, as seeming to be in conflict with the affirmation of his immutability.

On the first of these views that would reject the two-way understanding of reconciliation by declaring that man alone needs to be reconciled, much of what is said in the previous section of the need for God to be propitiated could be repeated here. It will, consequently, be enough to refer to two chapters on the 'Need, and 'Necessity of Reconciliation' which appear respectively in the works of Denney and Brunner. In our earlier volume, The 'Atonement of the Death of Christ', we observed that 'although their theologies differ in important respects', yet they focus 'alike on the radical nature of the atonement.'[3] Both see the necessity for reconciliation in the disturbing nature of sin which affects both God and man. Man's sin introduced mutual enmity into the relation between God and man. For Denney, 'The need of reconciliation is given in the fact of alienation or estrangement.'[4] Sin issues in guilt, and 'guilt alienates us from God, and it is in virtue of this alienation that sin reigns in us. Hence to be reconciled to God is the sinner's primary need.'[5] No less strongly does Brunner emphasise the estranging nature of sin: 'Sin alters the attitude of man to God and in doing so it alters the nature of man . . . The change introduced by sin, however, does not only affect men, it also affects God.'[6] Therefore, 'if any truth is obvious, certainly it is not forgiveness but punishment.'[7] Sin brings man under God's condemnation and makes him an object of his wrath. Only, therefore, 'where man recognises this reality of God's wrath does he take his guilt seriously; only then does he realise the personal character of God, and his own personal relation to him.'[8] Such is the condition brought about by man's sin in the relationship between God and man. Unless, then, God's wrath is turned aside none can be saved. Unless God becomes reconciled to man, man must forever bear the punishment of his sin and be swallowed up in the second death.

Nor is it proper to argue that, since God is love, no change of attitude is required on his part because of man's sin, for his love cancels out his wrath. This view is based on a false idea of the divine love. God's love is not just a mere love of benevolence; it is such a holy love that it is the very cause of his wrath against all evil. Yet it is a love that nevertheless is the source of his reconciling act (Rom. 5:8; 2 Cor. 5:14; cf. Eph. 2:4; 3:17). Therefore, the reconciliation is itself a revelation of God's holy love. It is a reconciliation that flows from God's changeless character as love. God's love is not purchased from his holiness by the Calvary event. The love of God must be seen for the divine reconciling reality that it is. It is all too easy for us to interpret the love of God by analogy with our human experience of affection. As P.T. Forsyth remarks,

> We treat all love as God's love by a certain juggle with the word divine. We seek the perfection of love in sacrifice instead of in redemption, in sacrifice for the beloved's good instead of sacrifice for the rebel's salvation. We identify renouncing love with redeeming love. We idealise reciprocal love, and call it divine, instead of reading God's revelation of his love as dying for the ungodly. This is love original and absolute. Hereby know we it at its source. If we translate let us translate from the original and not back from a translation. Let us work downward from love's own account of itself in Christ. Let us begin at the beginning, or, however we translate, at least let us interpret man by God, love by grace.[9]

It is in the cross of Christ, in the awful reality of the Calvary event, that the love of God is truly known. In the cross God's love has its completest action and its full display. It is his love which moved him to remove the barrier against man's sin which his holiness made inevitable. In the cross, in his righteous wrath against human sinfulness, God's full holiness in his earnest reaction against sin and God's full love to forgive the sinner intersected for man's redemption.

The other objection to the two-way nature of reconciliation is more theological and philosophical. It is argued that to admit 'change' in God would undermine the historic Christian doctrine of the divine immutability. But the God of the Bible is not a sort of static Monad. Rather is he presented and revealed as a personal being with all the properties of personhood in individual fullness.[10] Throughout scripture there is abundant evidence that God's attitudes do change to correspond to his moral action towards the changing character and conduct of men. This is not to say that there is any fickleness in God's nature. For there are those realities of his being which remain constant, and which persist through his manifold relationships with his created order. Behind his varying attitudes and actions which involve his change from friendship presupposed by reconciliation, there lies his unalterable holy nature and unwavering moral purpose which gives consistency and harmony to such attitudes and actions.

The idea of God in many historic dogmatics as a being of unchanging perfection is a creation of Greek philosophy rather than of biblical revelation. However, many recent philosophers of religion and theologians have recognised that 'change' as well as 'changelessness' - contingency as well as necessity, can rightfully be predicated of God. The philosophical justification of this doctrine has been well argued by Charles Hartshorne. He says, 'Not the Gospels and the Old Testament, but Greek philosophy was the decisive source for the Classical idea of the divine perfection.[11] Elsewhere he observes that the static conception of God as *actus purus*, having no potentiality and completely self-contained is an Aristotelian, and not a biblical conception. Hartshorne does not accept that change, conflict and suffering are characteristics unworthy of God.[12] He therefore rejects von Hugel's studied repudiation of patripassianism - the view, that is, that God the Father cannot suffer.[13] Von Hugel argues that God is too much our friend for us not to rejoice that he does not suffer. Hartshorne cannot see how a God who reveals sympathy can be without suffering. He prefers to think that sympathetic suffering is the highest form of personality; and most of all in God. And he asks, can God be indeed our friend and not suffer, and, could an impassible Deity be one in whom we could rejoice? Hartshorne does not think so. The world is not abstracted from its sufferings; and God has not abstracted himself from it. He thus concludes that, since God enters into relationships with his creatures, he consequently accepts relationships with his creatures, he consequently accepts relationship with the world's suffering.[14] It is our conviction that Hartshorne is right in his contention that there is evidence throughout scripture of what we have referred to elsewhere as the 'divine adaptability' in his dealings with men. God shows himself ready to do a new thing, to make again another vessel to replace the marred one.[15]

God's changed relation to man in reconciliation is in harmony and consistent with the unchanging nature of God as holy love. So the doctrine of the divine immutability cannot be invoked to deny God's changed relation to man, which the concept of reconciliation requires. For in the Calvary event God was not far off and Christ was not 'wrenching favour or forgiveness for men from a God who is reluctant to bestow it.'[16]

Accomplishment of Reconciliation

The other question to which answer is required is: how was the reconciliation accomplished? The answer to this question is already implied in the last statement of the previous section. Reconciliation is God's action in Christ as it is Christ's act for God. It is to Paul, as the apostolic preacher of reconciliation, that the church is indebted for the doctrine of reconciliation as it relates to man's salvation. Indeed, as James Denney says, 'It is he who describes what it is to be a Christian in the words 'we have received the reconciliation' (Rom. 5:10). It is he who says, 'All things are of God, who reconciled us to himself through Christ' (2 Cor. 5:18).'[17]

In three passages the apostle Paul expounds the gospel doctrine of reconciliation. They are brought together here so that we might the more readily understand what the doctrine affirms.

For if, when we were enemies, we were reconciled to him [God] by the death of his Son, much more, now that we are reconciled, shall we be saved by his life. Not only so, but we also rejoice in God through our Lord Jesus Christ, through whom we have now received reconciliation (Rom. 5:10, 11).

Therefore, if any one is in Christ, he is a new creation; the old has passed away, behold, the new has come. All this is from God, who through Christ reconciled us to himself and gave us the ministry of reconciliation; that is God was in Christ reconciling the world to himself, not counting their trespasses against them, and entrusting to us the message of reconciliation. So we are ambassadors for Christ, God making his appeal through us. We beseech you on behalf of Christ: be reconciled to God. For our sake he made him to be sin who knew no sin, so that in him we might become the righteousness of God (2 Cor. 5:17-21).

And you who once were estranged and hostile in mind, doing evil deeds, he has now reconciled in his body of flesh by his death, in order to present you holy and blameless and irreproachable before him' (Col. 1:21, 22).

In these collected passages there are nine occurrences of the term in one or other of its constructions; reconciled, reconciliation, reconciling. We must bring to its consideration the twofold understanding of the concept; that of God's reconciliation to men, and man's reconciliation to God. True, many modern commentators and theologians insist on the manward reference only. However, other able commentators and theologians are equally certain that the two-way reference is not only present in the word itself. but that its necessity is implied by its usage in the passages themselves. Denney, commenting on 2 Corinthians 5:18-21 notes the impatience shown by critics of the two-way significance of the term. 'Clever men have exhibited their talent and courage in calling it "heathenish"; and others have undertaken to apologise for St Paul by describing this objection as "modern".'[18] Denney expresses astonishment that, 'one should feel entitled either to flout the Apostle in this matter, or to take him under ones patronage'. And he is certain that,

> To St. Paul the estrangement which the Christian reconciliation has to overcome is indubitably two-sided; there is something in God as well as something in man which has to be dealt with before there can be peace. Nay, the something on God's side is so incomparably more serious that in comparison with it the obstacle on man's side simply passes out of view . . . . It is God's earnest dealing with the obstacle on His own side which constitutes the reconciliation.[19]

In this regard it would seem that even a cursory reading of the passages reveals that reconciliation is an act accomplished fully on God's side; and the word of reconciliation a reality to be accepted on man's side. On God's side reconciliation is God's own act. It was God, against whom man sinned and rebelled, who undertook the reconciliation. Man had brought about the condition of enmity and alienation which called forth the wrath and judgement of God. Yet it was God who took the initiative in the reconciliation. Thus, as we shall see, while the work of Christ was his reconciling commission, it was even more the function of the justice, the love, the glory. the power and the grace of God. It was, in other words, an act of very God. For God did not meet the reconciling necessities which brought about his changed relation to man because of man's sin by a deputy. Christ was man's substitute, not God's. 'All this is from God'. 'God was in Christ reconciling the world'; '[God] made him, to be sin who knew no sin'. It is, therefore. as though God 'were making appeal through us', to 'be reconciled'. It was God who 'reconciled [you] in His body of flesh by his death'. The Calvary event was God's saving deed. God was not 'at a distance far withdrawn' from the Calvary event. He was there present. He was there as the God of our salvation. He was there to effect a reconciliation, to bring about in himself that changed relation to sinners in which he shows himself just and the justifier of those who believe. At the place called Calvary God's holiness and love met for man's salvation: his holiness in judgement on man's sin and his love for man the sinner. Thus the event of Calvary is not only the way of man's reconciliation with God: it is also, if it can be so stated, the way of reconciliation within God himself of the 'tension' between the divine holiness and the divine love. The inner 'stress' in God between his holiness and love, his judgement and mercy, his wrath and grace, had its resolution in his reconciling act in Christ. In the event of Calvary God, whose wrath rebellious and alienated man deserved, tore something from his own holy heart of love and gave it for our reconciliation.

But whereas reconciliation has its origin in God, it has its accomplishment in the Calvary event. It is through his death; 'in his body of flesh by his death'; in him 'who knew no sin' and who of God was made 'to be sin' for us. Such was the means of our reconciliation. Only in this way and in this place was our reconciliation achieved. In his death Christ has met in their completest measure all the moral and spiritual requirements for God to reconcile sinners to himself. In his death Christ took upon himself the full weight of God's judgement on sin and in the very act revealed the fullness of God's forgiving love. To bring about such a reconciliation was the purpose of Christ's coming into history as the Father's beloved Son; and that purpose he accomplished 'in his body of flesh by his death' (Col. 1:22). Paul, putting himself among God's ambassadors on behalf of Christ, entreats men, 'be reconciled to God'. He thereupon declares immediately, indeed, abruptly, 'For he hath made him to be sin for us, who knew no sin; that we might be made the righteousness of God in him' (2 Cor. 5:21 AV). The absence of the conjunction 'for' in the Greek text serves to make his words the more impressive and solemn. The statement should be taken as an exposition of verse 14, 'one has died for all'. Being 'made sin', he 'died for all'. Here is the keystone to the arch of Paul's teaching on the reconciling significance of the Calvary event. Sinless that he was, he was yet made sin on our behalf. The words mean more than that he was made a 'sin-offering'. The term for a 'sin-offering' is distinct, while the parallelism with righteousness prohibits its reference here. It is Christ himself, the sinless one, who was made sin - actually and really made sin for us. Thus did he who was 'made sin' carry our guilt and bear sin's punishment.

Although unwilling himself to accept the apostle's teaching in 2 Corinthians 5:21, Hastings Rashdall allows that it

> can hardly mean anything but that God treated the sinless Christ as if he were guilty, and inflicted upon him the punishment which our sins deserved, and that this infliction made it possible to treat the sinful as if they were actually righteous.[20]

This is, indeed, what the text means, and it is what was brought to pass in the Calvary event in the sin-bearing act of the sinless Christ. Upon him the Lord laid the iniquity of us all; so was fulfilled in the deed of the cross the words of Isaiah 53:6-7. Isaiah's prophecy found historic actuality in the sacrificial death of Christ. Here is the mystery and miracle of Calvary; of the Christ who by God's act took upon himself all the responsibility of our sin and bore for us its condemnation, to bring us into union with himself in the righteousness of God. Such is the wondrous 'transfer' by which our reconciliation was effected - our sins for his righteousness.

For what other thing was capable of covering our sins than his righteousness? By what other one was it possible that we, the wicked and ungodly, could be justified, than by the only Son of God? O sweet exchange! O unmeasurable operation! O benefit surpassing all expectation! that the wickedness of many should be hid in a single righteous One, and that the righteousness of One should justify many transgressors![21]

On God's side this reconciliation as a divine act is an objective transaction; an accomplished fact; a work finished in the death of Christ. In Christ's being 'made sin for us' there is completed sin's atonement.

It is a reconciliation final in Jesus Christ and his Cross, done once for all, really effected in the spiritual world in such a way that in history the great victory is not still to be won, it has been won in reality, and has only to be followed up and secured in actuality.[22]

Such a reconciliation, complete and final in the Calvary event, has a claim on man's response. Paul regarded it as his apostolic commission (2 Cor. 5:19), as it is for every preacher of the gospel, to urge men to 'be reconciled to God' (2 Cor. 5:20). It remains for man to receive the reconciliation (Rom. 5:11; cf. Col. 1:22); and so be justified by the blood of Christ, and, consequently, 'saved by him from the wrath of God' (Rom. 5:9). The reconciliation achieved by Christ brings about within the responding life a transformation so complete that the believer becomes 'a new creation' (2 Cor. 5:17). As a result the sinner, forgiven and justified, is no longer in a state of enmity against God, no longer helpless and ungodly (Rom. 5:6). He is accepted into sonship in the righteousness of the Son of God's love. The love of God displayed in the death of Christ 'has been poured into our hearts through the Holy Spirit which has been given to us' (Rom. 5:5).

The use of the word 'counting' (RSV, NIV) or 'imputing' (AV) in 2 Corinthians 5:19 in the context of reconciliation shows that this concept does indeed overlap in some significant way with that of justification (cf. Rom. 5:9-10). For both doctrines, the idea of 'to reckon' is an essential factor (2 Cor. 5:9-10; Rom. 4:2f.). In reconciliation, however, in contrast to justification, the subjective element has prominence (2 Cor. 5:11-15). It is through the reconciliation achieved by Christ and in him that a sinner can come into joyous experience of acceptance by God. So says Denney:

> The question to be answered is not, 'What is Christ doing to reconcile men to God?', but, 'What did he do for this purpose in his life and Passion?' In other words, we are concerned here with what used to be spoken of as the finished work of Christ. The unfinished or progressive work - that which is still going on in the restoration of man to God - is, of course, not in dispute, only it is assumed that it proceeds on the basis of the other. The other - the finished work of Christ - what has just been described as the objective atonement, is precisely what is meant by *katallage* in the New Testament. It is on its completeness and finality that the finality and perfection of the Christian religion depends. It is this which justifies the evangelist when he says 'Receive the reconciliation' (Rom. 5:11). or, 'Be reconciled to God (2 Cor. 5:20).[23]

In summary, then, reconciliation may be defined as that act of God through Christ, whereby the alienation between God and man resulting from man's sinful rebellion is removed. As a consequence of his sin, not only was man's relation to God disrupted, but God was alienated from man, and man exposed to God's just wrath. It is not, then,

> our enmity against God that comes to the forefront in the reconciliation, but God's alienation from us. This alienation on the part of God arises indeed from our sin; it is our sin that evokes this reaction of his holiness. It is God's alienation from us that is brought into the foreground whether the reconciliation is viewed as action or result.[24]

In Christ, through his death, his physical death, God, the alienated one, brought into operation that factor which allowed him in justice to give place to his wrath and to receive man into the restored fellowship of the sons of God. 'All this is from God, who through Christ reconciled us to himself and gave us the ministry of reconciliation; that is, God was in Christ reconciling the world to himself, not counting their trespasses against them, and entrusting to us the message of reconciliation' (2 Cor. 5:18-19).

Racial Reconciliation

In two passages the wider reconciling significance of the Calvary event is given prominence. In Ephesians 2:13 it is declared that the Gentiles, considered by the people of Israel 'afar off' (beyond, that is. the pale of the chosen nation, cf. Isa. 49:1; 57:19; see Acts 2:39), have been brought near by the blood of Christ. Among later Jews the ceremony of receiving a proselyte was called 'making him near'. But Paul is saying here that Gentiles, who were not even 'near' as proselytes, are brought into 'nearer nearness' to God 'in Christ'. They are made thus near by the reconciliation effected 'by the blood of Christ' (cf. Eph. 1:7). Christ 'has broken down the dividing wall of hostility' (Eph. 2:14), 'by abolishing in his flesh the law of command- ments and ordinances' (v. 15), and has reconciled both Jew and Gentile' in one body through the cross' (v.16). Reconciliation is thus more than the reconciliation of God to sinners and sinners to God. It is racial as well, the reconciliation of Jews and Gentiles in Christ, whose purpose was to 'create in himself one new man in place of the two' (v. 15). The expressions used by the apostle in this section of Ephesians, 'the blood of Christ' (v. 13), 'in his flesh' (v.14) and 'through the cross' (v.16), are all different ways of referring to the Calvary event as the means of reconciliation. Every occasion of enmity, whether between God and man, or man and man has been done away by 'the blood', 'the flesh', 'the cross' of Christ. In this regard the statement of P.T. Forsyth is opposite, 'Reconciliation means the life-communion of the race.'[25] It is that because it is an aspect of reconciliation man is less ready to accept.

There is not a Christian Church or a Christian nation in the world which believes heartily in the Atonement as the extinction of privilege, and the levelling up of all men to the same possibility of life in Christ, to the same calling to be saints.[26]

For it is too tragic a fact that when men have not entered into reconciliation with God they fall apart and continue in their hostility. But it still remains for man to 'receive the reconciliation'. The primary form of reconciliation is that of the sinner to God. This first necessity carries with it the open possibility of the reconciliation of man with man, which is, as Denney says, 'a smaller but not a less attractive application of reconciliation, as accomplished in Christ's death.'[27] It is in their coming into right relationship with God that men and women discover their oneness in their new being as children of God. For such reconciliation of individuals creates the Church as one body in Christ (Eph. 2:14f.). For even though the passage is concerned primarily with the enmity between Jew and Gentile the context implies that their reconciliation was effected by the cancelling of the enmity between God and man occasioned by the law which made the Gentiles 'children of wrath' (Eph. 2:3).

Cosmic Reconciliation
The other statement which shows the wider significance of the reconciliation effected by Christ comes in Colossians 1:19-20 NIV: 'For God was pleased to have all his fullness dwell in him, and through him to reconcile to himself

all things, whether things on earth or things in heaven, by making peace through his blood, shed on the cross.' The NIV is certainly correct to interpret the 'in him' at the beginning of the verse as relating to God. By supplying the term 'God' as subject the reading of verse 20 runs on smoothly. Thus is the reconciliation of all things declared to be accomplished by God in the Calvary deed of Christ. In Christ, in whom all the fullness of the Godhead dwells, God has effected the reconciliation of the whole created order. The use of the term in 2:9, where Paul refers to 'the whole fullness of deity' settles the meaning here. It was the good pleasure of the Triune God that all the divine 'plenitude' should reside in Christ in bodily form (2:9). The words 'mean nothing else than all the divine fullness in its totality.'[28]

It is possible that the term 'fullness' was used by the heretical teachers of Colossae to refer to the totality of aeons and agencies which they supposed emanated from Pure Being. In this view the aeons were regarded as intermediaries between God and man, steps in a ladder which linked heaven and earth. Against such a theory, Paul presents the cosmic Christ as Lord of all. He portrays Christ as the one in whom all that is of God, by God's good pleasure, took up permanent residence and there dwells. (Such is the significance of the term in 1:19 - *katoikestai* - aorist, cf. Luke 13:4; Acts 1:20; Heb. 11:9; cf Matt. 23:21; Eph. 3:17). Paul's word

> undermines the whole of this theosophical apparatus in one simple, direct affirmation; the fullness or totality of the divine essence and power has taken up its residence in Christ. In other words, he is the one Mediator between God and mankind, and all the attributes and activities of God - his spirit, word, wisdom and glory - are displayed in him.[29]

If 'all plenitude' of Godhood took up abode in Christ in bodily form as the incarnate Son, then it may be certainly added that besides all the fullness of the Godhead that was in Christ, there was present in Christ also all the fullness of manhood. This reality of Christ's manhood is given significance in the declaration that he 'has now reconciled you in his body of flesh by his death' (Col. 1:21). Jesus Christ in the days of his flesh was truly man, fully man - the very perfection of manhood, 'yet, he knew no sin' (2 Cor. 5:21). In the incarnation of the Son of God manhood was enriched in Godhood; and by the resurrection and ascension, manhood was elevated to the throne of God.

It was not only the good pleasure of God that all fullness both divine and human should reside in Christ, the incarnate Lord, but that in him, besides, all things should be reconciled. As the plenitude of God's energy was manifested in his creative action in the pre-existent Word, so, too, is his reconciling activity manifested in the incarnate Word. Five times in the passage this cosmic significance is underscored by the use of the phrase 'all things'. Through him was the creation of all things; so, through him is the reconciliation of all things. 'The width of the reconciliation is the same as creation, they are coterminous.'[30]

It is the biblical view that at the Fall not only was man's nature affected by his sin, but the whole of creation itself was also disrupted (cf. Rom. 8:18-23, AV). The cosmic order became 'subject to vanity', but by God's act through Christ sin and its effects are measured and mastered. The universe is one reality, not only because it is created through the one personal divine Word of God, nor yet because it finds its principle of cohesion in him, but finally because, in ways past finding out, the reconciling power and grace of the Calvary event reach to its utmost depth and height. 'In reconciliation, as in creation, the work of Christ has a cosmic significance; as we are told in Eph. 1:10,11, it is God's eternal purpose to sum up all things in Christ.'[31]

Significantly, the order of the reconciling process is the reverse of that of the creative. When the creation is in view, the order is, 'in heaven and on earth' (Col. 1:16), the stated Old Testament order of creation. But, when speaking of reconciliation, Paul puts it the other way round, 'on earth or in heaven' (v. 20), as if to indicate that those things which stand closest to the redeeming cross are the first to experience the effects of its healing power.

Cosmic reconciliation is effected 'by the blood of the cross'. Such is the awesome cost of the restitution of all things; 'by means of the sacred blood which signifies and embodies his vicarious death, with its immediate merits.'[32] Contrary to the speculations of the false teachers, Paul traces the reconciliation of all things to the atoning work of the Calvary event (cf. Col. 2:14; Rom. 3:25; Eph. 1:7; 2:13; Heb. 9:12-14; 1 Pet. 1:19; 1 John 1:7; Rev. 1:5; 7:14; 12:11; see Gal. 6:12,14; Eph. 2:16; Phil. 2:8; Heb. 12:2). In his comments on the several passages in the New Testament in which the idea of reconciliation occurs, Matthew Henry contends that such reconciliation has its foundation in Christ, for He has 'paid the price for it.' In Him is found its promise and fulfillment being 'proclaimed' by him as a 'prophet', and 'applied' as a king.

Notes

1. Orr, James, (1909) 'Propitiation', in Hastings, J. (ed.) *Dictionary of Christ and the Gospels*, Edinburgh, T.& T. Clark, ii, 474.
2. Denney, J., (1911) *The Christian Doctrine of Reconciliation*, London. Hodder & Stoughton, 131, 132.
3. McDonald, H.D., 'The Atonement of the Death of Christ', in *Faith. Revelation and History* Grand Rapids, Baker, 272.
4. Denney, *op. cit.* 187.
5. *ibid.*, 191.
6. Brunner, E., (1934) *The Mediator*, tr. Wyon, O., London, Lutterworth, 463.
7. *ibid.*, 449.
8. *ibid.*, 445.
9. Forsyth, P.T., (1948) *God the Holy Father*, London, Independent Press. 59; quoted also in McDonald, *op. cit.*, 348, 349.
10. c.f. McDonald, (1986) *The God Who Responds*, Cambridge, James Clarke, ch. 1.
11. Hartshorne, Charles, (1962) *The Logic of Perfection and Other Essays in Neoclassical Metaphysics*, La Salle, Open Court, 34.
12. c.f. Hartshorne, C. and Reece, C., (1950) *Philosophers Speak of God*. London, 208.
13. c.f. von Hugel, F., (1926) *Essays and Addresses on the Philosophy of Religion*, London, Dent, 197f.
14. c.f. Hartshorne and Reece, *op cit.* 154f.
15. McDonald, The God Who Responds, 68.
16. c.f. Denney, *op. cit.*, 121f.
17. *ibid.*, 141.
18. Denney, (1980) *The Second Epistle to the Corinthians, Expositor's Bible*, London, Hodder & Stoughton, 213.
19. *ibid.*, 212.
20. Rashdall, Hastings, (1920) *The Idea of Atonement in Christian Thought*, London, Macmillan, 94.
21. *The Epistle to Diognetus.*
22. Forsyth, P.T., (1910) *The Work of Christ*, 77.
23. Denney, *op. cit.* 239.
24. Murray, John, *Redemption: Accomplished and Applied*, Grand Rapids, 34.
25. Forsyth, *op. cit.*, 94.
26. *ibid.*
27. Denney, J., (1911) *The Death of Christ*, (rev. edn), London, Hodder & Stoughton, 145.
28. Lohse, E., (1971) *A Commentary on the Epistle to the Colossians and Philemon*, ed. Koester, H., Philadelphia, Fortress Press.
29. Bruce, E.F. and Simpson, E.K., (1951) 'Commentary on Ephesians and Colossians', *New International Commentary*, ed. Bruce, Grand Rapids.
30. MacLaren. A., (1898) *The Epistle to the Colossians, Expositor's Bible*, London, Hodder & Stoughton.
31. Moule, H.C.G., (1898) *Colossians Studies*, London, Hodder & Stoughton.

Chapter XIV
ACTUAL REALISATION

The grand truth with which the two previous chapters have been concerned is that, in the Calvary event, Christ has secured for sinners the means of their redemption through the blood of his cross. It is so presented as a work done once-for-all, through which the obstacles created by man's sin in the way of his acceptance by God have been dealt with, and the way to his reconciliation made sure. The wrath of God on sinful humanity has been stayed in his loving cancellation of sin in the atonement of the death of Christ. Herein is the good news of the gospel; the ringing certainty that Christ has done for us all that was divinely necessary for our full salvation. Such is the objectivity of the atonement effected on Golgotha's tree which focuses the fact of Christ's work as complete and final. On the deed of the cross the full range of sin-affected reality, both human and cosmic, ultimately depends for reconciliation and restoration to God.

It is not our purpose here to particularise all the benefits that accrue to the natural order, or all the blessings that are available to humankind because of the Calvary event.

These issues, which belong, more properly, for detailed statement to a systematic theology, I have treated elsewhere.[1] It is enough for our present concern to consider in a summary manner the realisation of Christ's atoning act in human life; and, then, only such issues that relate more particularly to its declared effect in individual experience. We shall limit ourselves to those effects which focus for us the objectivity of Christ's work as distinctly the cause of the redemptive blessings apprehended within subjective experience. We affirm the essential inwardness of faith in the atonement, while, at the same time, declaring its absolute objectivity as a finished work. In this way the historic event of Calvary is brought into the realm of contemporary life. For the work of Christ, so experienced, lifts Christ's act above the space-time conditions of Golgotha. Christ's death as so apprehended is, then, more than a historical happening. For the Christ who in time died on a cross transcends time as the ever-living one, present for man's salvation through the historic deed of Calvary. That Jesus died is a certain fact of history. But to affirm in the commitment of faith that he died 'for me' is to pass beyond history and to be free of its power.

With James Denney we consider it then,
perhaps necessary to remark that when we speak of the finished
work of Christ we do not think of separating the work of Christ from
him who achieved it. The New Testament knows only a living
Christ, and all apostolic preaching of the gospel holds up a living
Christ to men. But the living Christ is the Christ who died. and he
is never preached apart from his death and from its reconciling
power. It is the living Christ, with the virtue of his reconciling death
in him, who is the burden of the apostolic message.[2]

The work of Christ is, then, a redeeming actuality, accomplished for us
while we were yet sinners and, consequently, subject to the wrath of God; but
it is a work, nevertheless, to be realised within contemporary human
experience. The Christ who dies for us must, in the efficacy of his reconciling
death, become effectual in us. What is needed, not, indeed, to complete
Christ's atoning deed, but to confirm its completeness, is the personal
commitment of faith's conviction, he 'loved me and gave himself for me'
(Gal. 2:20). Thus does the reality of Christ's finished work in the Calvary
event become actualised in Christian experience; and the power of God's
holiness and love, objective in the gospel of the cross, has its subjective
effect as the power of God's redemptive grace in the lives of 'us who are
being saved' (1 Cor. 1:18; cf. Rom. 1:16).

To realise in experience the accomplished work of Christ is. in the first
place, to be forgiven. There are two passages in the New Testament which
refer the subjective awareness of sin's forgiveness to the objective act of
Christ's death on the cross. The first of these is in Matthew's record of the
institution of the Last Supper. Taking up the cup Jesus bade his disciples
drink of it, saying, ' "This is my blood of the covenant, which is poured out
for many for the forgiveness of sins" ' (Matt. 26:28). The other passage
which links forgiveness with the death of Christ is Ephesians 1:7, 'In him we
have redemption through his blood, the forgiveness of our trespasses,
according to the riches of his grace'. The phrase 'in him' has, according to
T.K. Abbott, 'a certain argumentative force'. It emphasises the locale in
which alone the boon of God's forgiveness becomes ours. Only in Christ is
this possibility to be realised; for only he has paid the price by which
forgiveness of sin is assured. The price of our forgiveness 'in him' is
'through his blood'. This declaration affirms not only the means by which
our redemption, which is 'the forgiveness of our trespasses'. is secured, but
also the cost at which it is accomplished (cf. Rom. 3:24-25; 1 Pet. 1:18-19).

By stating that forgiveness is 'in Christ' and 'through his blood', the
person and work of Christ are brought together as the means of forgiveness.
There is no forgiveness apart from Christ, the Christ who in his death 'bore

our sins in his body on the tree'. The Calvary event is the place and way of our forgiveness, the sole medium through which a well-grounded assurance of its reality comes home to the trusting heart. All that went into the death of Christ, to appease in God his holy reaction against sin and manifest his antecedent love for sinners, was enacted that an absolute forgiveness might be made real and effective to believing sinners. In an earlier work, *Forgiveness and Atonement*,[3] we were concerned with the whole problem of forgiveness. There we discussed such questions as whether forgiveness of sin is really possible and why it should be maintained that forgiveness is assured only on the ground of Christ's atoning work. Here, however, only some general affirmations, in the context of our present theme, are required.

It is in the Calvary event that we can finally estimate the measure and depth of sin as it affects God. Only there do we learn of sin's true nature as an affront to the divine holiness and as open repudiation of God's loving fatherhood. It is thus only in forgiveness that man can be restored to that state of sonship in which to live and enjoy the presence of God. This 'means that forgiveness can only take place as a real divine act. The sense of acceptance, the certainty of forgiveness can only legitimately refer to a divine act of revelation, to an explicit communication of this divine secret'.[4] Therefore, H.R. MacKintosh can rightly declare,

> No man can properly be ranked as a Christian, in the sense of the New Testament, who has not received forgiveness of sins, or who is not conscious that through its impartation something has happened of decisive moment in his relation to God.[5]

This fact of forgiveness is, then, if not the sum, at least the secret of Christianity. It is, that is to say, the distinctive biblical revelation. There is no forgiveness in nature; for punishment, not forgiveness, appears as the inviolability of the natural order. Its possibility cannot, consequently, be deduced from natural religion. As John Owen says, 'the consideration of his [God's] works (i.e. nature) will not help a man to the knowledge that there is forgiveness with God.'[6] Other faiths may have their high ethical concepts of God, but they know little of a God who forgives, for they have no Calvary event to which to appeal as the ground of its certainty. So is it to be affirmed, 'the Christian doctrine of forgiveness is based upon the fact of atonement.'[7]

Echoing some thoughts from the last chapter of our *Forgiveness and Atonement* on the necessity of the atonement, note should be taken of how in a line in her hymn - 'He died that we might be forgiven' - Cecil Frances Alexander associates the death of Christ and the forgiveness of sins. So are related Christ's passion and God's pardon; the former being regarded as necessary to the latter, as in some way its ground and cause. Put specifically, this is to affirm that 'atonement is what it cost God to forgive the sins of the world'.[8] Therefore, P.T. Forsyth contends that in the light of New Testament teaching, 'Forgiveness through atonement is the essential of Evangelical Christianity.'[9]

It is thus a sure reading of the New Testament that divine forgiveness is the centre of our experience of God's salvation, and the atoning act of Christ is the basis of that forgiveness. The clear biblical truth is that were there no atonement there would be no forgiveness. There is a sense in which it can be truly asserted that only in such manner could God forgive. He could not simply declare forgiveness as a sort of universal amnesty. He could not just pronounce a general forgiveness and leave undealt with the cause and result of the sin that needs forgiveness. Such a declaration would not have brought about in man the condition for his acceptance by God. A forgiveness that is merely verbal is powerless to remove sin's guilt and cancel its legal sentence. Scripture is emphatic that God had to overcome something real in his relation to sinful humanity to reach man in forgiveness. In the light of God's holiness the absolute connection between God's wrath and man's sin must seem to render forgiveness impossible. The inevitable conjunction between human sin and divine judgement must mean that only by a miracle of his devising can God bring about sin's remission. In the cross, God's loving forgiveness of sinful man broke through the wrath of his judgement. The Calvary event is a real divine action, in which forgiveness had its validity and vindication in the deed of Christ's cross and in the truth of his person. The cross is thus divinely necessary as a way to the remission of sin. What Christ has done for us had to be done, if ever forgiveness was to be ours.

To be justified is a further realisation of the Calvary event in the realm of experience. 'Justified' is a Pauline term. In his exposition of the doctrine the two aspects, the objective and the subjective, are clearly stated. Justification by the blood of Christ (Rom. 5:9) points to its objective reality; 'therefore, since we are justified by faith' (Rom. 5:1) points to its subjective actuality. In his exposition of it Paul integrates the objective and the subjective aspects (cf. Rom. 4:5ff.).

Paul sets forth justification as an act of divine grace (Rom. 3:24). It is, none the less, a forensic act, since God in the Calvary event passed judgement on our sin in Christ our substitute, according to the measure of his wrath dictated by his holiness. So Paul sets forth justification as an act of God in the language of acquittal. The objective procurement of that acquittal rests on the fact that Christ took to himself man's sin, with all its guilt and condemnation; and its subjective realisation is in terms of the sinner's full acquittal by faith. It is on the ground of what God has done in Christ in the Calvary event that such as have faith are declared acceptable in his sight. Simply, therefore, to emphasise the character of justification as an experience, and to reject the view that *dikaiousthai* ('to justify') refers to the universal act of salvation accomplished at the cross, is to miss the fact that the act is always present as salvation, and therefore available for personal apprehension. This is, of course, necessary because when there is reference to *dikaiousthai, pistis* ('faith') is always included (Gal. 2:16; 3:8; Rom. 3:28; 4:5; 5:1). It is impossible to separate once-for-all justification at the cross from justification by faith.[10]

It is not our purpose here to enter on a full discussion of the doctrine of justification.[11] Our concern is rather to secure the fact that it is because of the Calvary event that man can stand as righteous in the presence of God in the righteousness of Christ. By faith in Christ's sin-bearing act the believer is caught up into the righteousness of Christ and declared acquitted of transgression. In that faith he is reckoned right with God. He has received a righteousness not of works (Rom. 4:4-5); that is, he has received God's 'free gift of righteousness' (Rom. 5:17). Jesus Christ's 'act of righteousness leads to acquittal and life for all men' (Rom. 5:18). Such is 'the righteousness from God that depends on faith' (Phil. 3:9; cf. Gal. 5:5).

In the commitment of faith the forgiven sinner 'is not one who is reputed to be, but in his very being as a believer actually is, right with God.'[12] For to believe in Christ and in his sin-bearing love revealed in him is to do the one right thing for which the situation calls. When the sinner does thus believe he does the one right thing, and it puts him right with God; in St Paul's language he is justified by faith. God accepts him as righteous, and he IS righteous; he has received the reconciliation (Rom. 5:11), and he IS reconciled.[13]

So is our justification altogether a matter of grace, and 'if it is by grace, is no longer on the basis of works, otherwise grace would no longer be grace' (Rom. 11:6). But the grace of God revealed in Jesus Christ through the blood of the cross is effective for everyone who puts his trust, not in his own righteousness by the works of the law, but in him who justifies the ungodly. The declaration, then, that a man is justified by grace through faith is for Paul the very core of the gospel (Rom. 3:24). 'Paul's doctrine of justification is his characteristic way of formulating the centre truth that God forgives believing sinners. Theologically, it is the most highly developed expression of this truth in the New Testament.'[14]

It is in his forgiveness that a man is justified; for the two are as one in faith's realisation of the Calvary event. So H.R. MacKintosh says, 'To be justified in the sense that counts for Christian experience is simply to be forgiven and accepted by God.'[15] Forgiveness is, then, to be conceived as the dynamic of justification: it is that act of God which makes justification credible. Forgiveness establishes a relationship which justification declares. 'The forgiven man craves to know his personal status before God. Justification is God's answer to his awakened conscience.'[16] It is this consideration which allows systematic theologians to discuss forgiveness of sins in the context of justification by faith. Some, like Thomas Watson, put forgiveness in the forefront of justification, and define the latter, consequently, as 'an act of God's free grace whereby he pardons sins, and accepts us as righteous in his sight, for the righteousness of Christ only, imputed to us, and received by faith.'[17] Others, like E.B. Redditch, virtually identify justification and forgiveness, and so speak of forgiveness as 'full restoration of fellowship with God.'[18] Louis Berkhof and Vincent Taylor, however, consider forgiveness as one element in justification. The former affirms forgiveness as a 'negative element' in the process;[19] while the latter declares justification 'more than remission of sins' though 'it implies and includes this gift of God.'[20]

From the standpoint of theological definition these discriminations may be allowed; but from that of the saving experience they have little meaning. God's forgiveness is certainly no mere negative affair. He does not, as it were, pronounce forgiveness from his enthroned remoteness and leave the pardoned sinner outside the door. It is the assurance of the Christian gospel that in his forgiveness the believer is admitted in Christ, on the basis of his atoning work, into immediate relationship with God himself (Rom. 5:1). Such as are forgiven in the grace of God's pardon are at once accepted as righteous and are brought into that fellowship with God through Christ by being made partakers of his holiness (Heb. 12:10); partakers of that holiness without which no man can see the Lord (Heb. 12:14). In God's forgiveness man is justified; and vice versa, in his justification he is forgiven of all his sin. And the

> basis of this verdict is the representative death and resurrection of Jesus himself. In view of universal sin, God can only be in covenant with human beings if that sin is dealt with, and this is achieved by God himself in the death of his son (Rom. 3:24-26; 5:8, 9). Jesus takes on himself the curse which could have prevented God's promised blessing finding fulfilment (Gal. 3:10-14). The resurrection is God's declaration that Jesus, and hence his people, are in the right before God (Rom. 4:24, 25).[21]

So in Acts 13:38-39 Paul, having stated the basic facts of Christ's death and resurrection, goes on to affirm, 'Let it be known to you therefore, brethren, that through this man forgiveness of sins is proclaimed to you, and by him every one that believes is freed [Justified' *dikaioutai*] from everything from which you could not be freed [literally, 'were not able to be justified] by the law of Moses.

It is thus that Karl Barth in a comment on Question 56 of the Heidelberg Catechism, 'What do you believe concerning 'the forgiveness of sins?' ', observes,

> To believe in the Holy Spirit is to hold to what happened for me in the death of Jesus Christ because of the humiliation of the Son of God. It is to believe that my sins are forgiven, that "for the sake of Christ's reconciling work, God will no more remember my sins ... so that I may never come into condemnation."[22]

It will be understood, then, why the sixteenth-century Reformers, in their zeal for the rediscovered biblical doctrine of justification, should strongly emphasise in their preaching and theological statements the objective side of God's saving act in the Calvary event. Yet it would not be true to charge that their teaching provided only a mere mechanical and external view of salvation, for it was not believed 'that the sinner could get along with justification alone.'[23] They were aware that the objective reality of salvation through the once-for-all act of God's holiness and love in Christ needed to be made effectual in human hearts. The salvation of God, secured on the cross of our Lord Jesus Christ, comes in creative power through the Spirit of God to those who make the response of faith. The subjective realisation of God's objective act accomplished in Christ assures, indeed, for the believer forgiveness and justification; and in that forgiveness and justification the believer is a 'new man' and a man redeemed. He is lifted into a new relation with the Father; he enjoys a new status in the Son; and he possesses a new nature through the quickening power of the Holy Spirit.

It is because of the 'blood of Christ' that all the redemptive blessings of God are realisable to faith's commitment. It is to the cross of our Lord Jesus Christ that all that belongs to our salvation is traced. Were there no shed blood of Christ, there would be no cleansing from sin's defilement. Were there no cross, on which the Prince of Glory died, there would be no atonement for sin; no reconciliation to God; no certainty of eternal life. But the shed blood and the cross are realities of the Calvary event. And these realities, finished objectively for us, are actualities to be completed subjectively in us. For such is the 'so great salvation' secured for sinners in the blood shed and the cross endured. At the high price of the Calvary event, yet as freely open to all who have faith, God has disclosed himself as the God of salvation.

Notes

1. McDonald, H.D., (1982) *Salvation*, Westchester 111. Crossway Books, chs. 4, 5, 6.
2. Denney, J., (1911) *The Christian Doctrine of Reconciliation*, London, Hodder & Stoughton, 287.
3. McDonald, H.D., (1984) *Forgiveness and Atonement*, Grand Rapids, Baker.
4. Brunner, E., (1934) *The Mediator*, tr. Wyon, O., London, Lutterworth, 449.
5. MacKintosh, H.R., (1927) *The Christian Experience of Forgiveness*, London, Nisbet, 2.
6. Owen, John, (1977) *The Forgiveness of Sins*, (reprint), Grand Rapids. Baker, 124.
7. Brunner, *op. cit.*, 516.
8. MacKintosh, *op. cit.*, 190.
9. Forsyth, P.T., (1909) *The Cruciality of the Cross*, London, Independent Press, 1.
10. Kittel, C. and Frederic, C., (1964-76) *The Theological Dictionary of the New Testament*, (tr. Bromley, G.W.) Grand Rapids, Eerdmans.
11 McDonald, *Salvation*. 94-109; *Forgiveness and Atonement*, ch. 5.
12. Denney, *op. cit.*, 291.
13. *ibid.*, 290.
14. Packer, J.I., (1990) 'Justification' in Douglas, J.D. (ed.)*The Illustrated Biblical Dictionary*, London, Inter-Varsity Press, ii, 842.
15. MacKintosh, *op. cit.*, 3.
16. Mullins, E.Y., (1917) *The Christian Religion in its Doctrinal Expression*, Philadelphia, Roger Williams, 54.
17. Watson, Thomas, (1960) *The Body of Divinity*, (3rd edn) London. Banner of Truth, 157.
18. Redditch, E.B., (1937) *The Forgiveness of Sin*, Edinburgh, T. & T. Clark, 514.
19. Berkhof, Louis, (1958) *Systematic Theology*, London, Banner of Truth, 514.
20. Taylor, V., (1952) *Forgiveness and Reconciliation*, London, Macmillan, 199.
21. Wright, N.T., (1988) 'Justification' in Ferguson, S.B. and Wright, D.F. (ed.) *New Dictionary of Theology*, Leicester, Inter-Varsity Press, 359,360.
22. Barth, K., (1964) *The Heidelberg Catechism*, tr. Guthrie, Shirley C., London, Epworth Press, 87.
23. Warfield, B.B., (1927) *Biblical Doctrines*, New York, Oxford University Press, 461.

Chapter XV
CHRISTOLOGICAL IMPLICATIONS

The foregoing pages will have made clear that, according to the testimony of scripture as the word of God, it is through Christ's sacrifice of atonement that faith apprehends the salvation of God. This truth of the gospel consequently puts Christ in some specific and unique relationship to God. For to affirm that there is divine redemption in Christ is one and the same with declaring God as the God of our salvation.

This consideration gives point to the oft-repeated statement that 'Christ is Christianity'. But that statement left unqualified is not, however, precise enough to characterise the distinctive nature of the Christian faith. For it must be immediately enquired, 'What Christ is the object of such Christian faith?' Not, certainly, the 'historical Jesus' of liberal New Testament criticism, its critical fancy, nor yet the Christ of much modern Christological thinking. The Christ of Christian faith and gospel is the total biblical Christ, not to be robbed of his essential place in the trinity of the Godhead, nor denuded of his accepted place in the conditions of manhood. A Christ so reduced could not effect an atonement sure and sufficient for our salvation. He who would take upon himself man's sin must be one with man in his human state, and he who would be for man the salvation of God must be one with God in his divine state. Therefore, for man to be redeemed by the action of Christ's atoning sacrifice offered for him is at one with his being forgiven by the action of God's saving grace proffered to him.

It is this understanding of the death of Christ that the New Testament puts at the centre of gospel faith. The cross has divine significance for man's salvation in the reality of his absolute deity, as it has historic accomplishment in the fullness of his human existence. A Christ less than God, or as an honorary God bearing a courtesy title, cannot perform what only authentic Deity can do. Brunner states what is a truism of biblical faith to begin his volume on the atonement, *Der Mitter*: 'Through God alone can God be known.' With equal certainty can it be stated as a biblical truism; through God alone can God redeem. For God is known to us supremely as God the Redeemer. Therefore, for redemption there must be atonement since 'Atonement is the foundation on which the experience (of redemption) is based.'[1] It is on this score that P.T. Forsyth can rightly affirm, 'the Godhead of Christ is a faith that grows out of that saved experience of the cross which is not only the mark but the being of any church.'[2]

It is in the light of the cross alone that a true estimate of the greatness of Christ can be made. If his position in relation to God is not unmistakable in everything that he said, it is surely inevitable in the thing he did. For, while his atoning sacrifice had its final effect on man, it had its first effect on God. And it had its first effect on God because of who Christ was in relation to God. Thus is Christology not only the corollary of soteriology; it is its condition and its reason. This means that the deity of Christ is at the centre of Christian faith, because it is the postulate of the redemption effected on his cross, and so is the essence of the gospel. The Christianity of the cross is not, then, to be reckoned among the religions of the world. Rather is it to be affirmed and accepted as a judgement on all religions as man's endeavour to gain access to God by his own methods and in his own way. Understandable, then, in this regard is the remark made by Deitrich Bonhoeffer in an address to his Barcelona congregation in 1927. He declared to them that, 'Christ is not the bringer of a new religion, but the bringer of God'. And in *The Cost of Discipleship* he again affirms, 'The disciple always looks only to his Master, never to . . . Christ and religion.'[3]

It is certainly the case that the apostolic exponents of the Calvary event would never have included his death as having significance for man's redemption if he had not himself done so. They would not have put Christ, and him crucified, in the centre of the Christian gospel if he had not first put himself there. It must, then, be categorically stated that during the days of his living among men Jesus knew himself commissioned of God for the fulfilment of a divine mission; and saw himself as commissioned, in the light of Old Testament prophecy, for the enactment of the messianic redemption. And he did convey to his disciples, in the measure that they could take it in, what was the God-ordained purpose of his presence among men. In their learning who he was they were also given some disclosure of what he came to do. And that 'something' he would do, as only he could do, for man's salvation, because of who he was in relation to the God of our salvation. It follows, therefore, that it is 'the doctrine of the atonement which secures for Christ his place in the Gospel, and which makes inevitable a Christology, or a doctrine of his person.'[4] Thus Christ's atoning work is the key to his nature, and the right interpretation of the cross the interpretation of his person. He, being in the form of God, humbled himself and became obedient to the death of the cross (Phil. 2:6f.).

Atonement for Sin

It was because Jesus lived among men as man should live, always in the light of God's presence, that he could undertake on man's behalf an atonement for man's sin. Therefore are his person and work one in the actuality of the atonement, so that, 'when we understand who he is we understand his work'[5]. It is, then, to be repeated again and again that it is *Christ*; the Christ who is presented to us in the whole New Testament revelation as at once historical and super historical and as human and divine; and *him crucified*, by the hands of wicked men and yet according to the counsel and foreknowledge of God - who is in the person that he is and in the death that he died, the essence of the Christian gospel. It is his existence and action as the God-man that constitutes his person and work as at once revelation and salvation. For in the last reckoning his revelation is the actualisation of salvation; and vice versa, his salvation is the focus of his revelation. Hence it is not the story of Jesus which is the object of Christian faith, but the disclosure of God in Christ's person and work as the one mediator between God and man: specifically and actually Christ as mediator in the unity of his person and work in the atoning event of Calvary. For to 'lay the stress of Christ's revelation elsewhere than on the atoning cross is to make him no more than a martyr, whose testimony was not given by death, but only sealed by it.'[6]

Christ's death cannot be conceived as a noble example of a martyr to a cause. As we have declared elsewhere:

Jesus did not die merely as another volunteer in the regiment of the heroic. His death belongs to anther category altogether. For 'Christ died for the ungodly' (Rom. 5:6); 'while we were yet sinners Christ died for us' (Rom. 5:8); 'for Christ died for sins once for all' (1 Pet. 3:18).[7]

Christ's death was not a seal on his work. It was truly his consummate work which gathered in it his whole person. Christ did not go to the cross of Calvary to declare an example or to prove a point. He went there to do something; something absolute and decisive, which altered on God's part his relation to fallen humanity and to a sin-disturbed world.

In his triumphant cry as he died, ' "It is finished" ' (John 19:30) or, as the one Greek word, *Telelestai*, can be translated, 'the work is done', it is affirmed that Christ in his death has accomplished fully in its every requirement the purpose for which he had come, namely, to give his life a ransom for many. In the Calvary event he exposed sin in all its sinfulness and bore it in his own body to the tree, to open up the way whereby God could, in love, forgive sin in righteousness. Christ 'brought forgiveness as the son of God alone could, as God forgiving, as forgiveness incarnate, as one actually redeeming and not offering redemption, as the divine destroyer of guilt; as the Eternal Salvation of God, made historic and visible.'[8] In the event of the cross the redemption of God was made actual and final, by being made thus 'historic and visible'. For that death was not just a testimony to the good things Jesus went about doing, and at such a cost to himself because of his loyalty to some high conviction. It was an atoning death which consummated his whole ministry and assured that it was a sinless life he offered and poured forth on Calvary's tree.

Between Christ's death and his saving work there is, then, a vital connection. If, therefore, there is divine forgiveness assured to man at all, it is realised solely on the grounds of the atoning act of Christ in the blood that he shed for the remission of sins. Thus does the Apostles' Creed declare the fact of Christ's suffering - 'he suffered under Pontius Pilate', and belief in the forgiveness of sins - 'I believe in the forgiveness of sins', and so links the two realities, Christ's suffering in the Creed is intended to focus on it as having a significance for Christian faith beyond the fact he participated in the sufferings that belong to our human condition; or even, in his case, that his was a fate altogether undeserved because he himself was innocent of any punishable offence. The truth is that, as the Creed would have it concluded he died for our sins that we might know the forgiveness of God. So is the cross a revelation in time of God's eternal nature as holy, yet forgiving, love.

The cross in human history is a consequence and not the precondition of the cross in the heart of God (cf. 1 Pet. 1:20; 2 Tim. 1:9; Rev. 13:8). God was already forgiving and loving before the sacrifice on Calvary, but his forgiveness had to be realised and manifested on the plane of history in the momentous event of the crucifixion. His love could not have been made available for his children until his holiness had been satisfied concretely in history. The cross, therefore, signifies both the judgement of God on sin and the love of God on sinners.[9]

The sufferings of Christ were certainly brought about by man, but their inner and divine meaning for man's salvation was realised in God's action in the crucified one.

Throughout the New Testament there is constant affirmation of relationship between the death of Christ and man's sin. It is made quite clear that had not Christ in the Calvary event borne in our stead the burden of its guilt, death and curse, we would most surely perish. In the last analysis consequently, it is only in reference to God that sin is understood for the terrible reality that it is. Sin, in its essential nature and result, is the disturbance of the personal relationship between God and man. Its final evil is that it is repudiation of God; a rejection of his fatherly authority and love in the ordering of his way in a world created for man's good. So is man's sin the derangement of his existence in relationship with God and of the moral order in which the actuality of his living to glorify God could be fulfilled.

To be sure, man himself does not regard sin as such, for it belongs to the nature of sin to conceive of itself as no great issue. Social and political idealism declare man's greatest need to be deliverance from suffering, ignorance and want. Those that have a religious origin and retain a religious flavour allow the need for the individual to be emancipated from the bondage of material gain. In some quarters today, Christianity itself is presented as a programme for human betterment, social change and economic sharing. 'But all this is seldom traced back to the one root; sin against God, personal guilt, from which we can only be released by forgiveness.'[10] By his sin man has severed the unseen ties which bound him in a relationship of obedient and loving fellowship with God. So must it be declared: 'Sin is full of the sense of wrong towards God.'[11] It is not mere disregard of some legal enactment, not a transgression of some ethical code. 'Against thee, thee only, have I sinned', confessed the psalmist (Ps. 51:4) of his own sin, to focus the reality of all sin. In substance sin is an attitude of resistance to God; in result it is a fact of moral perversion which merits the judgement of God.

But the most serious factor about sin is that it is not just a matter of evil acts. Sin is a reality of man's fundamental nature; a condition of his own deep-down being. Man is a sinner of himself and in himself. Everyman can say truly of himself, 'myself am sin'. Thus, before God, man's nature has become spoiled and perverted. And from man as sinner the holiness of God must recoil. As he is, man cannot stand, indeed, could not hope to stand, within the presence of such a God who is 'of purer eyes than to behold evil and canst not look on wrong'. (Hab. 1:13). Before God, therefore, the whole world is guilty. Because of man's repudiation of his original relationship between himself and his creator, guilt now lies between God and man. 'This sense of being wrong with God, under his displeasure, excluded from fellowship, afraid to meet him, yet bound to meet him, is the sense of guilt'[12].

The sense of guilt is a universal fact of human existence; the feeling that, when a wrong is done, it should not have been done. A bad conscience is a witness to man that the evil to which he has given expression has its origin and cause in himself. Furthermore, the existence of conscience is a common property of all human life. And conscience, in Hamlet's words, 'doth make cowards of us all'. Paul associates conscience with man's native moral sense (cf. Acts 23:1; 24:16; Rom. 2:15; 9:1; 13:5). Possessing this natural faculty a man can judge whether or not his own actions accord with his innate moral awareness (2 Cor. 1:12). Conscience 'presents man as his own judge.'[13] Dietrich Bonhoeffer stresses this self-judging role of conscience in reference to the commonly held view that conscience is the voice of God. Conscience, according to Bonhoeffer,

pretends to be the voice of God and the standard for the reaction to

other men. It is, therefore, from his right relation to himself that man
is to recover the right relation to God and to other men, and so comes
to a knowledge on his own account of good and evil.[14]

The upshot of this obedience to conscience is that it can lead a man to
the utterly false idea that he has reason for boasting of his moral integrity as
ground for his acceptance with God.

The call of conscience in the natural man is the attempt on the part
of the ego to justify itself in its knowledge of good and evil before
God, before men, and before itself, and to secure its own continuance
in self-justification.[15]

But the real place of conscience is not in its justification of right conduct
for in any fulfilment of right conduct, the whole self acts. It is conscience that
stimulates a man to awareness of all sense of sin and guilt. To do wrong gives
us a bad conscience, and a bad conscience speaks more specifically of our
need of divine redemption from sin and release from its guilt. 'The bad
conscience makes definite the fact of our being wrong with God - of being
estranged from Him by what we have done, yet unable to escape from Him,
at once alienated and answerable.'[16] It is the fundamental truth with which
we have to deal, that a bad conscience, or a sense of sin, induces moral
paralysis.

It disables the moral nature on every side. It dulls moral intelligence,
so that unless we get delivered from it the practical reason or moral
sense becomes *nous lookimos*, a reprobate mind (Rom. 1:28), as Paul
has it; or in the terrible words of our Lord, 'the light that is in us becomes
darkness.'[17]

But while it is, doubtlessly, right to insist that the consequence of our sin,
in the awareness of guilt, is realised through conscience, it is to be stressed
at the same time that God's judgement of sin in his wrath is not enshrined with
this awareness. Some moralists and theologians contend that the guilt that
follows a wrong act is, like a hangover, itself its punishment. But this is to
overlook the fact that the consequences of evil actions go far beyond the
subjective awareness of the guilt incurred. Conscience cannot be isolated
from the moral order, or be thought to operate in a vacuum.

It is through his conscience that he [man] belongs to the moral world
and can conceive such an idea as that of punishment; but though it
is true to say that all punishment is through conscience, it is quite
unreal to say that it is limited to conscience.[18]

A bad conscience is, indeed, a fitting response to God's reaction to sin;
but a bad conscience is not the measure of the guilt that accompanies it. Sin
brings about guilt, real and actual, that is independent of it. Such guilt is no
mere subjective feeling. It is objective in the sense that it is a consequence

of man as sinner and finds expression in conscious acts of evil. On the guilt which has expression in evil acts of man as sinner, and as the sinner responsible for his evil; the wrath of God abides (cf. Rom.3:23,5:12 etc; Rom.3:19 etc; Rom.1:18,2:5; Eph.2:3; Col.3:6; 1 Thess.2:16 etc).

Forgiveness and the Cross

It is not, therefore, the 'education of conscience' that is our supreme human need; nor yet even

> the absorption of our sin, nor even of our reconciliation alone, but of our redemption. It is not cheer we need, but salvation, not help, but rescue, not a stimulus but a change, not tonics but life. Our one need is a moral need in the strictest holiest sense. The best of nature can never meet it. It involves a new nature, a new world. a new creation. It is the moral need not to be transformed but to be saved.[19]

For this salvation the one all-inclusive hope for man is the certainty of the divine forgiveness. And the real, and only, bridge head from which this saving reality can be assured is not the education of conscience but the act of Christ in the Calvary event. For, contends Kierkegaard,

> the forgiveness of sins is the great renewal that Christianity brought into the world. "Thy sins are forgiven thee." (Luke 7:48). that is the cry of encouragement of the Christian one to another; with this cry Christianity spread all over the world, by these words it is recognised a race apart, a separate nation.[20]

Such forgiveness cannot, however, be taken for granted as if there was some sort of moral necessity in God to bestow it. Nor is it the case, as Socinius was fond of asserting, that God's forgiveness of sins is a *sine qua non* of his 'pure benignity'. His proposed dilemma - that if God forgives sins freely he does not forgive on the basis of satisfaction, he does not forgive sins freely - does not meet the case. His antithesis comes to shipwreck on the fact of the apostolic preaching of Christ and him crucified; on the clear and decisive statements of the New Testament that he died for us and that he shed his blood for the remission of sin. All apostolic preaching focuses on the living Christ as the one who died that we might be forgiven: and the gospel is never preached apart from that death as the ground and certainty of God's forgiving grace.

In truth, only in the cross can God's forgiveness be taken seriously. Apart from the cross there is no reason at all to proclaim the forgiveness of God. Indeed, as Brunner says, 'forgiveness is the very opposite of anything which can be taken for granted';[21] and, again, 'But if any truth is obvious it is certainly not forgiveness but punishment.'[22] Neither nature nor the natural law can be appealed to as witnesses to forgiveness as a necessary cosmic moral principle. Forgiveness has no place in either. It is not the case that there is something automatic about God's forgiveness nor that there is some 'must' which compels him to do no other. Indeed, as John Owen says, 'Mercy and pardon do not come forth from God as light from the sun, or water from the sea, by a necessary consequence of their natures, whether they will or will not.'[23] Therefore, since God is the holy Creator of all nature and the source of the total moral order, forgiveness must be 'the great moral paradox, the greatest incredibility of moral life, needing all the miracle of Christ's person and action to make us realise it when we grasp its terms.'[24]

God is not to be conceived as a benevolent despot so sure of his position that he can afford to forgive the indiscretions of his subjects in order to gain their love and regard. Nor is he to be presented, which is the more likely idea nowadays, as an indulgent father who turns a blind eye to the doings of his erring children, accepting their excuse that to err is human. And if, perchance, one should feel guilt for a wrongdoing and confess, one would receive a ready pardon making a promise to try not to transgress again. God is not to be conceived after this fashion - neither as a benevolent despot nor an indulgent father. He is not to be patterned after our poor idea of the God we would like him to be. 'To whom then will you liken God, or what likeness compare with him?' (Isa. 40:18). not, certainly, to the likeness of a dumb lifeless image or yet to a medley of human concepts. For, in relation to both, Barth's affirmation applies, God is the 'Altogether Other'. To whom can we liken God? To his own revelation in Christ. To what likeness can we compare him? - to his one saving act in the deed of the cross.

It is in Christ, and him crucified, that God is known for the God that he is; the God of holiness and love; of justice and mercy. For in the cross the 'tension', between his rightness to exercise punishment of sinful humanity and his love for that humanity he created for fellowship with himself, was resolved. In the cross the right of God in his holiness to punish sin and the right of God of his love to forgive sinners found their fullest satisfaction. So was man's forgiveness of his sins in the grace of God's love secured on his behalf, in a manner consistent with his righteous judgement of sinful mankind, and in accord with ultimate moral principles of righteousness. In this sense, then, as Denney remarks:

> In forgiving sins, it might be said, God takes sides with us against Himself; He has a right to exact something from us, and for our sakes forgoes that right. His justice impels him in one direction, and His mercy in another, and in this very act of pardoning men and reconciling them to himself He must reconcile these two divergent attributes.[25]

It must be said, therefore, that atonement is necessary for man's salvation; necessary if God remains just and the justifier of all that believe. The work of Christ is a divine necessity for God to be true to himself and to the moral order that he has established in the world for the living of mankind as created in his image; that sin, in the very process in which it is forgiven, should also, in all its reality and fullness be borne. And it is the faith of the gospel, the disclosure of the biblical revelation that Christ in the Calvary event rendered satisfaction to these divine necessities. So is the cross the way, and the only possible way, in which God's absolute holiness and God's absolute mercy could be made actual for man's salvation. For

the cross demonstrates in fullest measure the wrath of God against sin and its endurance by the Son of his love. Christ in his work felt sin as it was felt by God and bore for man God's holy judgement of it. Justice as the law of God's holiness in relation to sin was meted out on Christ. The law's demand for sin's judgement, far from being lessened, had rather in the cross its completeness of action. God did not - indeed, could not because of his holiness - slacken the law's requirement or lighten sin's penalty. Both had in Christ their fullest scope and exaction. In the cross the holy Christ took all our sin, in all its sinfulness and in himself brought it under the holy judgement of God.[26]

The work of Christ was thus altogether a divine act; all that humanity did in the Calvary event was to crucify the Lord of glory; all that man contributed to it was that sin by which his redemption from its reality and guilt was secured. Such is the miracle of our salvation, the inconceivable fact, known to faith as a divine revelation: a salvation secured in such a way that the holiness of God, the inviolability of the moral law and the demand of the penal order were maintained. In the atoning cross there came to their ultimate expression the reality of the divine wrath on man's guilt and the reality of God's saving love for sinners. Thus it is said,

When Christ did what he did it was not human nature doing it, it was God doing it. That is the great, absolutely unique and glorious thing. It is God in Christ reconciling. It was not human nature offering its very best to God. It was God offering His very best to man.[27]

Therein lies the final necessity of the cross for man's salvation: a necessity which reveals God for what he is in relation to human sin. God himself, with whom sin cannot dwell, while maintaining inviolate the moral constitution of the universe, took all the sin of mankind and made his own beloved Son every sin for us; to bear its punishment, its curse and death. This he did for us and on our behalf, that we might be made the righteousness of God in him and be restored to the fellowship of sonship. Without that Calvary event, that holy deed of a loving God, there would be no forgiveness, no salvation for man. This one absolute and divine necessity for our redemption from sin; for the just appeasement of God in his holy anger against sin, and for his reconciliation of sinners of himself - Christ satisfied in his atoning cross. So is God's redemptive act in Christ of necessity consistent with his essential nature as holy love. For equally expressed in the Calvary event are his holiness in his judgement on sin in the suffering of Christ, and his love for sinners in the mediation of Christ. God would not be true to himself if he did not judge sin in wrath; nor would he be true to himself if he did not forgive sinners in love. In the death of Christ both the justice and love of God had their fullest actuality, to make the Calvary event a sacrifice acceptable to God and an atonement absolute for man.

Thus, while the work of Christ was his commission, it was even more, in a specific sense, the function of the justice, the glory, the power, and the grace of God as expressive of his fundamental being as Holy Love. Without this reality of the atoning cross Christianity would indeed be but another one of the world religions. But the great thing, the truly distinctive thing, about the gospel is that in the Calvary event there is settled once and for all the issue between a holy God of love and the sin of man. There is then nothing artificial about the Calvary event in relation to sin. It has not the character of a hurriedly devised scheme to meet an unexpecting happening. It is the one divine way, the only fitting way of our salvation. It has all the character of God in it.

Notes

1. Guthrie, Donald, (1981) *New Testament Theology*, Leicester and Downers Grove, Ill., 508.
2. Forsyth, P.T., (1909) *The Person and Place of Jesus Christ*, London, Hodder & Stoughton, 29.
3. Bonhoeffer, D., (1959) *The Cost of Discipleship*, London, SCM. 154.
4. Denney, James, (1911) *The Death of Christ*, (rev. edn), London. Hodder & Stoughton, 231.
5. Brunner, Emil, (1934) *The Mediator*, tr. Wyon, O., London, Lutterworth, 599.
6. Forsyth, P.T., (1907) *Positive Preaching and Modern Mind*, London, Hodder & Stoughton, 357.
7. McDonald, H.D., (1985) 'The Atonement of the Death of Christ', in *Faith, Revelation, and History*, Grand Rapids, Baker, 354.
8. Forsyth, *Positive Preaching*, 253.
9. Blotsch, Donald, (1978) *Essentials of Evangelical Theology*. San Francisco, Harper and Row, i, 166.
10. Brunner, *op cit.*, 515.
11. McDowell, Stewart A., (1932) *Is Sin Our Fault?*, London, Hodder & Stoughton, 210.

12. Denney, *The Death of Christ*, 279.
13. Westcott, B.F., (1892) *Commentary on Hebrews*, London, MacMillan, 292.
14. Bonhoeffer, Dietrich, (1955) *Ethics*, London, SCM, 149.
15. ibid., 211,212.
16. Denney, James, (1911) *The Christian Doctrine of Reconciliation*, London, Hodder & Stoughton, 190.
17. *ibid.*
18. *ibid.*, 215.
19. Forsyth, *Positive Preaching*, 56.
20. Kierkegaard, Soren, (1944) *Concluding Unscientific Postscript*, tr. Swanson, David and Lowrie, Walter, Princeton, N.J. Princeton University Press, 95.
21. Brunner, *op. cit.*, 448.
22. *ibid.*, 449.
23. Owen, John, (1977) *The Forgiveness of Sin*, (reprint) Grand Rapids. Baker, 92.
24. Forsyth, *Positive Preaching*, 290.
25. Denney, *Christian Doctrine of Reconciliation*, 21,22.
26. McDonald, *op. cit.*, 246,247.
27. Forsyth, (1910) *The Work of Christ*, London, Hodder & Stoughton, 24.

BIBLIOGRAPHY

Athanasius, *Against the Arians*, i
    De Incarnatione, iv
Barth, K., *The Heidelberg Catechism*, tr. Guthrie, Shirley, C., London, 1964
    The Epistle to the Romans tr. Hoskyns, Edwyn C., Oxford, 1933
Beckwith, C.A., article in Hastings, J., (ed.) *Dictionary of the Apostolic Church*,
    Edinburgh,
    1915
Berkhof, L., *Systematic Theology*, London, 1958
Blotsch, D., *Essentials of Evangelical Theology*, San Francisco, 1978
Bonhoeffer, D., *The Cost of Discipleship*, London, 1959
    Ethics, London, 1955
Bruce, E.F., and Simpson, E.K., "Commentary on the Ephesians and Colossians", *New
    International Commentary*, ed. Bruce, E.F., Grand Rapids, 1951
Brunner, E., *The Mediator*, tr. Wyon, O., London, 1934
Bultmann, R., *The Theology of the New Testament*, London
Calvin, J., *Commentaries on the Epistle of Paul to the Romans*, tr. and ed., Owen, John,
    Grand Rapids, 1947
    The Institutes of the Christian Religion, tr. Beveridge, H., London, 1940
Clements, J.C., "Passover", in Hastings, J. (ed.), *Dictionary of the Apostolic Church*,
    1915
Cross, F.L., *First Peter*, London, 1954
Delitzsch, A.F., *Commentary on Isaiah*, (ET) Edinburgh
Denney, J. *Studies in Theology*, 3rd edn, London, 1985
    The Christian Doctrine of Reconcilliation, London, 1911
    The Death of Christ, rev. edn, London, 1911
    The Second Epistle to the Corinthians, Expositor's Bible, London, 1980
Dodd, C.H., *The Bible of the Greeks*, London, 1935
    The Epistle of Paul to the Romans, London, 1935
    The Johannine Epistles, The Moffatt New Testament Commentary, London, 1946
Driver, S.R., "Propitiation", in Hastings, J. (ed.), *Dictionary of Christ and the Gospels*,
    Edinburgh, 1906
Edersheim, A., *The Life and Times of Jesus the Messiah*, London, 1897
Fensham, F.C., "Covenant", in Douglas, J.D. (ed.)*Illustrated Bible Dictionary*, London,
    1990
Forsyth, P.T., *God the Holy Father*, London, 1948
    Positive Preaching and Modern Mind, London, 1907
    The Cruciality of the Cross, London, 1909
    The Person and Place of Jesus Christ, London, 1909
    The Work of Christ, London, 1910

Godet. F., *Commentary on Romans*, Edinburgh, 1883
  Commentary on St. John's Gospel, (ET) Edinburgh, 1899
Gough, M., *The Origins of Christian Art*, London, 1973
Guthrie, D., *New Testament Theology*, Leicester, 1981
Hanson, A.T., *The Wrath of the Lamb*, London, 1959
Harrison, R.K., "Blood" in Tenney, M. C., (ed.), *Zondervan's Pictorial Encyclopaedia of the Bible*, Grand Rapids, 1975
Harshortne, C. and Reece, C., *Philosophers Speak of God*, London, 1950
Hartshorne, C., *The Logic of Perfection and Other Essays in Neoclassical Metaphysics*, La Salle, 1962
Hill, D., *Greek Words and Hebrew Meanings: Studies in the Semantics of Soteriological Terms*, 1967
Irenaeus, *Adversus Heresus*, iii
Jeweth, P.J., "Death" in Tenney, Merril C., (ed.), *Zondervan's Pictorial Encyclopedia of the Bible*, Grand Rapids, 1975
John of the Cross, *The Spiritual Canticle and Poems of St. John of the Cross*, tr. Peers, E. A., London, ed. 1978
Jungel, E., *God as the Mystery of the World*, tr. Guder, Darrel L., Edinburgh, tr. 1983
Kierkegaard, S., *Concluding Unscientific Postscript*, tr. Swanson, D. and Lowrie, W., Princeton, 1944
Kittel, C. and Frederick, C., *The Theological Dictionary of the New Testament*, tr. Bromley, G.W., Grand Rapids, 1964-76
Leighton, R., *A Practical Commentary on the First Epistle of St Peter*, London
Lightfoot, R.H., *St John's Gospel: A Commentary*, Revised Edition, ed. Evans, C.F., Oxford, 1956
Lohse, E., *A Commentary of the Epistle to the Colossians and Philemon*, ed. Koester, H., Philadelphia, 1971
Luther, M., *Works*, ed. Pelikan, J. and Lehmann, H.T., St Louis, Concordia. Philadelphia
MacKintosh, H.R., *The Christian Experience of Forgiveness*, London, 1927
MacLaren, A., *The Epistle to the Colossians*, Expositor's Bible, London, 1898
Martin, R.P., *Colossians, The Church's Lord and the Christian's Liberty*, Grand Rapids, 1972; Exeter
McDonald, H.D., "Biblical Teaching on Personality" in Jonnes, S. L. (ed.), *Psychology and the Christian Faith*, Grand Rapids, 1986
  "The Atonement of the Death of Christ", in *Faith, Revelation and History*. Grand Rapids
  Forgiveness and Atonement, Grand Rapids, 1984
  Salvation, Westchester, 1982
  The God Who Responds, Cambridge, 1986
  I and He, London, 1966
McDowell, S., *Is Sin Our Fault?*, London, 1932
Morris, L., *The Apostolic Preaching of the Cross*, London, 1955
  The Atonement: its Meaning and Significance, London, 1965
Moule, H.C.G., *Colossians Studies*, London, 1898
Mullins, E.Y., *The Christian Religion in its Doctrinal Expression*, Philadelphia, 1917
Murray, J., *Redemption: Accomplished and Applied*, Grand Rapids
Orr, J., "Propitiation", in Hastings, J. (ed.), *Dictionary of Christ and the Gospels* Edinburgh, 1909
  "Ransom", in Hastings, J. (ed.), *Dictionary of Christ and the Gospels*. Edinburgh, 1909

Owen. J., *The Death of Death in the Death of Christ*, ed. Goold, W. H., London, ed. 1959
    The Forgiveness of Sins, reprint, Grand Rapids, 1977
Packer, J.I., "Justification" in Douglas, J.D. (ed.), *The Illustrated Biblical Dictionary*,
    London, 1990
    Knowing God, London, 1973
Pink. A.W., *The Attributes of God*, Cleveland
Platt. F., "Propitiation", *Dictionary of the Apostolic Church*, Edinburgh. 1915
Rainey. A.F., "Sacrifice and Offerings", in Tenney, M.C. (ed.), *Zondervan's Pictorial
    Encyclopedia of the Bible*, Grand Rapids, 1975
Rashdall, H., *The Idea of Atonement in Christian Thought*, London, 1920
Redditch, E.B., *The Forgiveness of Sin*, Edinburgh, 1937
Ritschl. A., *The Christian Doctrine of Justification and Reconciliation: The Positive
    Development of the Doctrine*, ed. MacKintosh, H.R. and Macauley. A.B., Edin-
    burgh, 1900; New York
Robertson, A.T., *Word Pictures in the New Testament*, New York, 1930-33
Simpson, E.K. and Bruce, F.F., *Commentary on Ephesians and Colossians, New
    International Commentary*, ed. Bruce, F.F., Grand Rapids, 1951
Smeaton, G., *The Apostle's Doctrine of the Atonement*, Grand Rapids, 1957
Spurgeon, C.H., *Twelve Sermons on the Passion and Death of Christ*. Grand Rapids,
    1975
Stewart, J., *A Man in Christ*, London, 1935: reprint 1941
Stibbs, A., *The Meaning of the term "Blood" in the New Testament*. London
Stott, J., *The Cross of Christ*, Leicester
Tasker, R.V.G., *The Bible Doctrine of the Wrath of God*, London, 1951
Taylor, V., "Justification" in Ferguson, S.B. and Wright, D F. (ed.), *New Dictionary of
    Theology*, Leicester, 1988
Temple, W., *Readings in St John's Gospel*, London, 1914
Tertullian, *Adv. Marcionem*, ii
    De Carne Christi
Theilicke, H., *The Evangelical Faith*, ed. and tr. 1974-82 Barber, C.C. and Bromiley,
    G.W., Grand Rapids, 1978 Edinburgh
Tillich, P., *Systematic Theology*, Chicago, 1951-63, London
Trumbull, H.C., *The Blood Covenant*
van Gemeren, W.A., "Offering and Sacrifices in Bible Times", in Ewell. W.A. (ed.), *The
    Evangelical Dictionary of Theology*, Grand Rapids
von Hugel, F., *Essays and Addresses on the Philosophy of Religion*. London, 1926
Wallace, R. S., *The Atoning Death of Christ*, London, 1981
Warfield, B.B., *Biblical Doctrines*, New York, 1927
    Christian Doctrines, New York, 1920
Watson, T., *The Body of Divinity*. 3rd Edition, London, 1960
Westcott, B.F., *Commentary on Hebrews*, London, 1892
    Gospel of St John, London, 1900
    The Epistle to the Hebrews, London, 1890
    *The Victory of the Cross, Sermons Preached During Holy Week, 1888 in Hereford
    Cathedral*, London, 1888
White, R.E.O., *Broadman Bible Commentary*, ed. Allen, C. J., Nashville. 1979

INDEX OF
BIBLICAL REFERENCES

Genesis
2:17 — 40
4:4 — 84
6:18 — 73
8:20 — 84
9:9 — 73
9:10 — 73
9:11 — 73
9:13 — 73
9:15, 16 — 73
15:18 — 73
17:2 — 73
22:8 — 61
22:13 — 84
24:17 — 73
31:44 — 73
32:10 — 73
40:11 — 79

Exodus
3:7 — 17
12:11 — 71
12:13 — 71
12:15 — 70
12:17 — 70
12:18 — 69
15:13 — 73
18:20 — 70
20:6 — 84
21:30 — 90
23:18 — 71
24:6 — 8, 69, 82
29:14 — 85
29:17 — 85
29:39ff — 60

Leviticus
4:3 — 87
4:14 — 87
4:26 — 87
4:28 — 87
4:35 — 87
5: 5f — 27
6:30 — 105
8:15 — 105
9:12 — 85
14:10 — 59
16:20 — 105
17:11 — 45, 82
17:14 — 45
23:12 — 59
23:18 — 59
25:51 — 90

Numbers
4:33 — 25
6:14 — 59
11:1 — 98
21: 4f — 20
21:8-9 — 15
28:19 — 59
29: 2 — 59
29: 8 — 59
30:29 — 59
32:32 — 59

Deuteronomy
7:9 — 73
7:12 — 73
11:17 — 98
12:23 — 45
18:18 — 94

21:23 — 9, 26, 27
32:4 — 99

II Samuel
1:23 — 92

II Kings
11:17 — 73
22:17 — 98

II Chronicles
23:16 — 73
28:11 — 98
29:10 — 98
29:24 — 105
30:16 — 71

Nehemiah
1:5 — 73
9:32 — 74

Job
2:4f — 53
9:33 — 92
13:27 — 23
33:11 — 23
33:23f — 91
33:24 — 90, 91
33:26 — 91
33:28 — 91

Psalms
2:11 — 98
22:16 — 14
23:5 — 29

25:8 — 29
40:6-9 — 52
49:7f — 91
49:7 — 90
51:4 — 131
59:18 — 90
77:9 — 103
116:13 — 33

Proverbs
6:35 — 90

Ecclesiates
8:8 — 15

Isaiah
35:10 — 90
40:18 — 134
42:6, 7 — 75
43:3 — 9
43:25 — 18
49:1 — 114
49: 8 — 75
51:10 — 90
51:11 — 90
51:17 — 29
51:22 — 29
52:13 — 75
53: — 21, 25, 27
53:4 — 27
53:5 — 25
53:7 — 60, 112
53:10 — 75
52:12 — 55
57:19 — 114

Isaiah continued
59:20 72
61:1 63
Jeremiah
25:15f 29
25:17 29
31:11 90
31:31-34 75
31:31 76
31:34 18, 77

Ezekiel
45:15 105
46:13 50
17:20 105

Daniel
9:24 105, 6

Hosea
13:14 90

Habakkuk
1:13 131
2:9 39
2:16 29

Zephaniah
3:5 99

Malachi
3:1 73

Matthew
1:21 8
4:1f 14
4:9 17, 106
5:9 106
5:24 106
5:48 106
6:12 106
6:14 106
6:15 106
6:24f 106
7:21f 106
9:15 73

9:20 14, 47
11:28 106
13:54f 94
14:36 14
16:16 24, 35
16:21 24, 35
18:10-14 106
20:17-19 77
20:28 77, 78, 83, 89, 91, 107
21:19 78
21:38-39 35
23:21 116
26:28 43, 44, 48, 75, 77, 79, 83, 86, 120
26:39 29
26:47 23
27:21 17
27:51 17
27:53 53

Mark
1:1 7
1:14 99
1:15 106
2:10 75
3:5 99
8:3 38
10:43 39
10:45 78
12:8 78
14:3 30
14:12 70
14:24 24, 44
14:36 29
14:43 23
14:48 23
15:26 17
15:34 31, 32

Luke
1:67f 76

1:68 89
4:16f 14, 75, 82, 106
6:19 14
6:35-36 106
7:48 133
8:19 14
10:18 39
13:4 116
15:12ff 106
17:35 38
20:15 78
22:7 70
22:20 43, 44, 85
22:42 29
22:52 23
22:31 23
23:34 15
23:35 15
23:46 15, 32
23:47 15
24:21 18, 89
24:44-49 36, 107

John
1:2 62
1:10 62
1:20 59
1:35 59
2:12-13 60
3:14-15 20, 107
3:29 78
4:22 82
6:53 55
8:12 62
8:28 20
9:5 62
10:11 79
10:18 15
10:18f 15
12:24 21, 35
12:33 35
12:34 20
12:49 77
14:17 62

14:24 94
15:18 62
16:13 24
16:33 44
17:14 94
17:17 94
18:11 15, 33
19:6 15
19:11 15, 24
19:20 129
19:36 60, 70
19:37 15
21:15 63

Acts
1:20 116
2:23 23
2:39 114
3:14 99
3:19 18
5:30 23
8:29 59
8:32 59
10:36 105
10:39 35
10:40 24
13:28-29 23, 24
13:38-39 124
13:30 24
16:24 22
20:28 43, 48
23:1 131
24:16 131

Romans
1:16 120
1:18 99, 133
2:5 99, 133
2:15 84, 131
2:16 123
3:8 123
3:24 89, 92, 120, 122, 123, 124,

Romans continued
    133
3:25   48, 85,
    87, 92,
    97, 100,
    101,
    102,
    117,
    120,
    124,
    133
3:28   123
4:2f   113
4:4, 5   123
4:5ff   122, 123
4:15   99
4:17   38
4:24-25   125
5:1   105, 122
5:2   55, 56, 113
5:6   37, 39, 92, 113, 129
5:8   37, 81, 92, 101, 108, 129
5:9   37, 43, 47, 48, 87, 100, 122
5:10   36, 37, 110
5:11   113, 114, 123, 124
5:12   38, 133
5:21   25, 38
6:5   37
6:10   37, 92, 100
6:23   38
6:23   38

7: 6   70
7:13   31
7:23   100
8:1   25, 33
8:3   17, 56, 88
8:18-23   117
8:20   6
11:6   123
11:15   101
13:5   131
14:15   37

I Corinthians
1:17-18   16, 120
1:18   18
1:20   89
1:22   19
1:23   7, 35
1:30   56, 59, 70
5:7   39
6:11   56
7:23   92
10:16   33, 81
11:25   33, 48, 85
11:26   37
11:27   44
15:3   24, 33, 36
15:26   40
15:27   44
15:55-56   40
23:12   23

II Corinthians
1:12   131
1:18   18
1:20   76
5:2   19, 27, 38, 94, 112, 116
5:11   113

5:14   108
5:17   70, 110
5:18   107, 110, 114
5:20   107

Galatians
1:4   81
1:11   35
1:12   9
2:20   9, 18, 19, 37, 120
3:1   21
3:13   19, 23, 26, 32, 75, 77, 100
3:15-17   74
3:29   76
4:4   54, 76
4:28   76
5:11-12   16
6:9   100
6:12-14   117
6:14-16   21

Philippians
2:6   19, 128
2:7   65
2:8   16, 19, 36, 39
2:11   19
3:9   123
3:18   15

Ephesians
1:7   43, 44, 77, 79, 81, 89, 92, 115, 117, 120
1:10-11   117

1:14   89
2:3   115, 133
2:4   108
2:9   116
2:13   43, 87, 105, 114, 117
2:16   16, 17
2:17   105, 108, 116
2:18   53, 56
3:12   43
4:22   70
4:24   70
4:30   89
5:2   81
5:14   115
5:26   44

Colossians
1:14   56, 60
1:20   16, 17, 37, 43, 81, 105
2:1   117
2:9   54
2:13   18
2:14   15
2:15   17
2:16   107
3:6   133
5:18   107

I Thessalonians
1:10   72, 99
2:16   99, 133
2:21   77
5:10   39
5:23   44

II Thessalonians
2:7   18

I Timothy

2:5, 6	92
2:6	89, 91
5:6	94
6:16	38

II Timothy

1:9	120
1:10	38, 40

Titus

2:14	89

Hebrews

1:8	82
2:14	38, 152
2:17	97, 107
3:1	54
3:11	99
4:3	99
4:16	56
5:6	82
5:9	65
7:22	47, 75
7:24	54
7:27	77
8:6	75, 92, 95

8:8	75
9:5	105
9:7	47
9:12	14, 48, 117
9:13	44, 56, 87
9:15	44, 75, 88, 95
9:15-20	48
9:16-18	74, 75
9:22	43, 82
9:24	56, 82
9:26	77, 87
9:28	55, 77, 87
10:5	52, 87
10:10	55, 82, 87, 124
10:12	54, 56, 82, 88
10:14	56, 82
10:17-18	56
10:19	43
10:19-22	76
11:4	84
11:9	116
12:2	19
12:14	124

12:24	47, 75, 94
13:11	88
13:12	44
13:20	48, 79

I Peter

1:2	44, 63, 82, 88
1:3	25
1:18	89
1:19	25, 43, 44, 48, 59, 63, 69, 82, 88, 95, 117
1:25	9
2:19-25	25
2:22	19
2:24	23, 79
3:15	44
3:18	19, 25, 33, 39, 77, 88, 129

II Peter

2:24	19

Revelation

1:5	44, 64, 65, 117
2:7	25
5:6	25
5:8	25
5:9	35, 64, 65, 89
5:12	25, 62
6:1	25
6:16-17	99
7:14	65, 117
11:8	99
12:9	39
12:11	44, 117
12:12	39
13:8	25, 65, 130
14:10	29
15:3	99
16:19	29
18:12	23
19:9	73
19:15	99
20:2	20, 39
22:1	25, 64
22:2	25
22:3	66
22:19	35